Butterflies
OF ALABAMA

Glimpses into Their Lives

PHOTOGRAPHS BY **Sara Bright**

TEXT BY **Paulette Haywood Ogard**

THE UNIVERSITY OF ALABAMA PRESS ✦ TUSCALOOSA

Publication supported in part by the City of Selma, Alabama's
Butterfly Capital. A tip of the hat to Selma's Butterfly Lady, Mrs.
Mallieve Breeding.

Library of Congress Cataloging-in-Publication Data

Ogard, Paulette Haywood.

   Butterflies of Alabama: glimpses into their lives / Paulette
Haygood Ogard; photographs by Sara Bright.

     p. cm. — (Gosse nature guides)

   Includes bibliographical references and index.

   ISBN 978-0-8173-5595-1 (pbk. : alk. paper) 1. Butterflies—
Alabama. 2. Butterflies—Alabama—Identification. I. Bright, Sara. II.
Title. III. Series.

   QL551.A2033 2010

   595.78'909761—dc22   2009047778

In memory of Scooter
—PHO

For Tommy, Ben, and Emory with love
—SCB

Lepidoptera were my "first love" in Natural History.

—Philip Henry Gosse, as quoted in *Glimpses of the Wonderful: The Life of Philip Henry Gosse*

Contents

Preface

Glimpses of Alabama's butterfly populations have been few and far between. In 1838, Philip Henry Gosse was a young English naturalist on the brink of a renowned career. His eight-month foray into Dallas County left us with exquisite watercolor depictions of its common butterflies. Painted with homemade squirrel's hair brushes, his likenesses are minutely accurate and luminously beautiful. Gosse's "letters" or essays are as delightful as his sketchbook. Accounts of swallowtails, sulphurs, and satyrs almost fly off the page, and Gosse's descriptions of the local butterfly population provide an intimate peek into the natural world of nineteenth-century Alabama: "An eye accustomed only to the small and generally inconspicuous butterflies of our own country . . . can hardly picture to itself the gaiety of the air here, where it swarms with large and brilliant-hued swallow-tails and other patrician tribes, some of which, in the extent and volume of their wings, may be compared to large bats. These occur, too, not by straggling solitary individuals; in glancing over a blossomed field or my prairie-knoll, you may see hundreds, including, I think, more than a dozen species."[1]

Little more than a century later, Ralph L. Chermock provided a midtwentieth century look at our state's butterflies. Chermock, a biologist who was a specialist in butterfly classification, joined the faculty of The University of Alabama in 1947. The following year he agreed to serve as a regional reporter for the Lepidopterists' Society, filling a gap in the newly formed group's coverage of the southeastern states. When not mentoring students like E. O. Wilson, he and his wife Ottilie avidly sought butterflies in many states. Their collection, comprised of 30,000 specimens, is currently housed at the Alabama Museum of Natural History. Chermock's reports provide a textual snapshot of the times. A 1952 Season Summary strikes familiar chords regarding Alabama's fluctuating wet/dry weather patterns while making us yearn for the day when "at wet patches along the dirt roads" swallowtails, sulphurs, and crescents "would rise in clouds when disturbed" and Gorgone Checkerspots were among the rarer species that "flew in increased numbers and were fairly abundant."[2]

In this book, we offer our own glimpses into the lives of Alabama's butterflies. It is our hope that they will inspire closer looks that will more clearly define and delineate population dynamics, distributions and ranges, and life-history mysteries.

Acknowledgments

It has been a long journey from the time we initially decided to explore the relationship between native butterflies and plants to the publication of this book. Many people have given direction and guidance along the way. Without them, a project of this magnitude would not have been possible, and we are deeply grateful.

Year after year, Jan Midgley generously gave a wealth of information about native plants.

Winston and Linda (and Muffin) Baker went above and beyond to help with many species, especially the Diana Fritillary and the Texan Crescent.

Irving Finkelstein patiently shared his vast knowledge of lepidoptery with two very fledgling butterfly enthusiasts.

Barry Hart was invaluable to our research of the Alabama population of Mitchell's Satyr.

Many others shared information about specific butterflies, caterpillars, plants, habitats, and/or locations. Some offered encouragement at just the right time. Others provided support that kept our lives going. We thank them all, including James Adams; Frank Allen; Tom Allen; Cleo Bagwell; Missy Bates; the Birmingham Audubon Society; Richard Boscoe; Fay and Garland Bright; Hazel Bright; Bob and Mary Burkes; Vitaly Charney; Buck and Linda Cooper; Forrest Edwards; Bill Finch; Mary Ann Friedman; Tom Gagnon; Ben Garmon; Jeffrey Glassberg; Howard Grisham; John and Rosa Hall; Greg Harbor; Scott Hartley; JoVonn Hill; Richard Holland; Dan Holliman; Mike Howell; Sharon Hudgins; Henry Hughes; Jerry Jackson; Melanie Johns; Helen Kittinger and the Tuesday Girls; Robbie Limerick; Carol Lovell-Saas; Harry LeGrand; Gini Lusk; Joe MacGown; Jeffrey Marcus; Brian Martin; Mary Jo Modica; Gary Mullen; Chris Oberholster; Ricky Patterson; Harry Pavulaan; Buzz Peavey; Joni Pepper; Russell Perry; John and Denise Phillips; Andrew Rindsberg; David Roemer; Merritt Rogers; Mark and Holly Salvato; Dale Schweitzer; Dee Serage; Linda Sherk; Al and Linda Shotts; Jack, Millie, and Josh Rudder; Dan Spaulding; Keith Tassin; Bob and Ann Tate; Nigel Vinters; David Wagner; Jeanne and Lee Walls; Lori Wilson; Paulson, Lillie, Parker, Natalie, and Josh Wright.

Paulette's parents, Hoyt and Virginia Logan, have supported this project for at least five decades. Early on, they spent hours searching for butterflies with an inquisitive child. Later, they planted a butterfly garden, scoured their property for host plants, and spent hours searching for butterflies with an inquisitive adult. They proofread the entire manuscript. Their love and encouragement have been unwavering.

Logan and Mac Haywood put up with host plants in the car and caterpillars in the kitchen with patience and humor. And Bill Ogard never complains about the butterfly trips. Thanks, guys!

Peggy Haywood Hair wore many hats including that of field trip companion, proofreader, and Paulette's sister-in-law.

Carolyn Jackson, Marsha Perry, and Karen Rogers have tutored, critiqued, encouraged, and best of all, kept photography fun for Sara. Their expertise and friendship over the decades has been a treasure.

Sara's siblings and their families have supported this project in many ways ranging from field trips to child care to encouragement. They are Jim, Ramona, James, and David Lee Cunningham; David, Laura, and Dave Cunningham; Charles, Mary (stand-in mom when Sara is out of town), Catherine, Anna, and John Beck. The boundless support from her too-many-to-name, unusually close extended family has been wonderful. Thanks and love to all.

Jeanne and the late Emory Cunningham, Sara's parents, enjoyed nature and encouraged conservation. Their family spent time in the woods, and it is not surprising that her brothers, sister, and Sara are all apples that fell close to the tree in their love of and concern for Alabama's natural heritage. Times spent in the woods with her parents while working on this project are cherished memories.

Sara's husband, Tommy, has been invaluable to this work with his technical support. He has kept cameras and computers running, no easy task.

He has also designed a Web site to record data on Alabama butterflies, an even harder task. He has done these things and ever so much more with a constant good nature! Additionally, Tommy, Ben, and Emory Bright have been on many butterfly field trips. They have planted, packed, unpacked, searched, fed, watered, waited, built, and generally joined every phase of this adventure with enthusiasm most of the time and encouragement all of the time. Endless thanks and love to each.

Butterflies
OF ALABAMA

The Focus

Butterflies

The pages of this book are filled with images of butterflies. They draw our eyes and capture our attention. But what exactly are these creatures that we find so compelling? For at least two hundred years, taxonomists have answered that question by first defining general characteristics and then systematically moving toward the more specific. Generally, butterflies are insects—according to Linnaean taxonomy, members of the class Insecta. Their bodies are comprised of three segments: head, thorax, and abdomen. They are covered with an exoskeleton made of chitin, a tough organic compound. Six legged, compound eyed, and cold-blooded—regardless of all the ethereal characteristics we attribute to them—butterflies are insects.

More specifically, butterflies, along with moths, belong to the order Lepi-

Pearl Crescents on Butterfly Milkweed

doptera. Their diaphanous wings are covered with minute scales—touch them and powdery flakes will stick to your fingers. Lepidopterans undergo complete metamorphosis: their life cycle is made up of four distinct stages: egg, larva (caterpillar), pupa (chrysalid or cocoon), and adult. Unfortunately, the characteristics that distinguish butterflies from moths are not so clearly delineated. In Alabama, butterflies are often brightly hued, daytime fliers, while moths are drab and active at night. But anyone who has spent much time in the field realizes that there are many exceptions: satyrs are classified as butterflies, but they often fly well after dusk with wings that are monochromatic shades of gray and brown. And there is a whole group of day-flying moths, many of which are very colorful. A look at lepidopteran antennae is somewhat more conclusive. Butterfly antennae are filaments, knobbed or hooked at the tip. Moth antennae may be feathery, pencil thin, or tapered, but they do not swell at the end.

The knobby-antennaed lepidoptera classified as butterflies are further divided into three groups called "superfamilies." One superfamily (Hesperiidae) contains small, heavy-bodied lepidoptera called skippers. Traditionally considered butterflies, some taxonomists now believe they are more closely aligned with the moths. Another superfamily (Hedyloidea) is comprised of American butterfly-moths: a small neotropical group, formerly classified as moths, but now considered to be butterflies. Adding to the confusion, members of a third superfamily (Papilionoidea) are simply called "butterflies" (or sometimes "true" butterflies). Typically small bodied and proportionately large winged, they also have classic antennal clubs (rather than the hooked antennae of the skippers). These "true" butterflies are the focus of this book—most specifically, those that occur in Alabama, a state so biologically diverse that we believe eighty-four species live and breed within its borders during some part of a typical year.

Butterflies and Plants
Even glimpses into the lives of butterflies must include plants, for they are the primary source of food, shelter, and reproductive sites. Butterflies are

so intimately and inextricably dependent on the plant kingdom that adults, eggs, caterpillars, and chrysalides have their own special ties to it.

Many *adult butterflies* depend on flower nectar as their primary food source. But even those whose proboscis length relegates them to nonfloral foods often sip from decaying fruits or sap flows. One species, Zebra Longwing, eats pollen in addition to drinking nectar.

Butterflies also depend on plants for protection and shelter from the elements. Often-asked questions are, "Where do butterflies go when it rains?" and, "Where do butterflies spend the night?" Plants are a crucial part of the answer. Butterflies typically seek the cover of wind-breaking, rain-diverting plants during storms. They nestle under bark or in the cover of leaves to escape the cold. They roost in trees at night or deep in the cover of grasses.

Protection from predators is as essential as protection from the elements, and butterflies not only hide from them in plants, they often look like the plants in which they hide. Leafwings are well named because their underwings closely resemble dried foliage, but many other butterfly species also bear cryptically colored, leaf or bark-like undersurfaces that allow them to disappear with the close of a wing. Some are even shaped like plant parts. The elongated palps (or mouthparts) of the American Snout look like the petiole of a leaf.

Butterfly *eggs* are virtually always placed on plant material. Ovipositing females require the detection of certain phytochemicals to stimulate egg laying, and they bypass nonconforming surfaces. For many, even the presence of the correct chemicals is not enough to ensure placement of an egg. The perfect spot must be painstakingly located, and depending on the species, may mean positioning ova near the site of next season's bud or on the tender growing tip of fresh foliage—intricately tying the life cycle of the butterfly to the life cycle of the plant.

Caterpillars are consummate herbivores. With the exception of one species,[1] they dine solely on vegetable matter. But plants have developed an incredible array of defenses in their own fight for survival. Armed with hairy leaves, sticky sap, and ant-luring false nectaries, their arsenals can also in-

Comma Anglewing caterpillar's shelter constructed from False Nettle leaves

clude chemical warfare. Collectively they are filled with enough oils, acids, alkaloids, and tannins to fill a toxicology textbook. Butterflies and their caterpillars have countered with their own detoxification adaptations, and each species has found a culinary niche that is uniquely its own. Some are food plant generalists, able to partake from a wide variety of mildly toxic plant families. Others are strictly specialists—so highly adapted to a particular chemical array that they will eat no other. In an ironic twist, some butterflies have taken the proverbial lemons and made lemonade—they incorporate toxic phytochemicals into their own bodies and become poisonous (or at least unpalatable) to those that would eat them.

Larvae are even more dependent on plants for shelter and protection than their adult counterparts. Leaves are all important to many species. Not only do they eat them, they hide under them, in them, and on top of them. Sometimes they shape them to meet their needs. Caterpillars are very practical architects. They roll leaves into tubes, silk them together for nests, devise flaps and troughs, and add frass chains to their tips. Most of those that overwinter are protected by some part of a plant.

A look at the *chrysalides* of various butterfly species quickly reveals their close relationship to the plant kingdom. Many resemble furled leaves, while others appear to be broken twigs. The Falcate Orangetip's chrysalid looks exactly like a wickedly sharp thorn. And Hackberry and Tawny Emperor chrysalides so closely resemble the color and pattern of hackberry leaves that their host affiliation is undeniable. Although many caterpillars wander from their host plants before selecting a spot to pupate, most eventually dangle from other branches, twigs, or blades to accomplish their final molts. Some head for ground litter—usually composed of various types of plant detritus.

Butterflies and Predators

Butterflies and plants are in the foreground of our glimpses, but predators lurk in the background. They come in all shapes and sizes, attack from all fronts, and devour butterflies in every stage of their life cycle. Birds, frogs, and lizards; spiders, dragonflies, and praying mantises; ants, predatory wasps, and tachinid flies all readily make meals of butterflies, eggs, larvae, and pupae. Predators may be outside our range of vision, but their presence is undeniable, and their effect is dramatic. The outward appearance and behavior of butterflies is often a response to the need to escape this predatory presence.

The most obvious way to avoid a predator is to be impossible to catch. Butterflies are equipped with four wings that enable them to make aerial getaways. Swallowtails are powerful fliers; their remarkable tails increase their stability when gliding. Hairstreaks dart and satyrs bounce, but both present erratic, difficult-to-grab targets. Caterpillars lack wings, but sometimes even they seem to take to the air, dropping out of sight and dangling by a thread when threatened.

Predators cannot eat what they cannot find, so many butterflies become invisible. We have already discussed the highly effective coloration that allows adult butterflies to resemble leaves, lichen, and bark, and how some caterpillars hide in leaf shelters. A host of caterpillars and chrysalides have also perfected the art of camouflage. Many are leaf green, and some are bark brown. Larvae that eat blossoms and buds are often colored to match them. Various stripes, dots, and chevrons help to create optical illusions. Countershading is common: the top surface is lighter than the bottom, which enables larvae to blend into the shadows. Other patterns create the effect of leaf, needle, or flower texture. Some caterpillars remain hidden by getting rid of revealing signs of their locations. They may discard incriminating droppings (or frass) by flinging it far away with the flip of an abdomen or the toss of a jaw. Others clip the stems of partially eaten leaves so that telltale evidence falls safely to the ground.

Another way to avoid becoming a meal is to taste so bad that no one wants to take a bite. Because of the toxic plant substances they ingest, some caterpillars are distasteful or sickening to higher-level predators like birds, reptiles, and amphibians. Many retain these qualities into adulthood. But toxicity is only an effective survival tactic if would-be consumers are aware of the threat to their gullets. Butterflies advertise their indigestibility with

Opposite: Monarch clutched by Praying Mantis

bright warning (or aposematic) colors. Classic color combinations are red, orange, and white, typically combined with an accent of black. While aversion to these signals may be based on learning, evidence also exists that some predators innately recoil. Regardless, a broad look at butterfly populations reveals that adults, larvae, and even eggs colorfully flaunt the fact that they are unpalatable, figuratively yelling, "If you eat me, I'll make you sick."

Not all butterflies taste bad enough to gag a predator, but some achieve the next best thing—they look like those that do. In Alabama, Pipevine Swallowtail mimics are classic examples. Their caterpillars eat toxic pipevine (or aristolochia) plants and become poisonous in their own right. Even as adults they retain the trait, and as many as six butterfly species mimic their black-and-blue winged, orange-spotted appearance.

In addition to mimicking inedible butterflies, throughout their life cycles, many butterflies mimic other inedible objects. Feces are a favorite, because excrement is almost universally shunned as a food source. Swallowtail and admiral caterpillars look remarkably like bird droppings, sometimes so shiny that they appear to be wet.

Some caterpillars mimic predators. Many of the same swallowtail caterpillars that begin life in dung disguises transform into small snake or tree frog mimics as they mature. Brightly colored osmeterial glands even resemble a snake's tongue. A hungry bird may be startled enough to pass on making a snack of the tiny copycat.

Butterflies and caterpillars even imitate parts of themselves. Front-to-back mimicry is common, particularly among the hairstreaks and the swallowtails. Antennae-like tails and nearby hindwing eyespots combine to create the illusion of an additional head. Confused predators often snap at the wrong end, allowing the unharmed butterfly to escape with only a little wing damage. Some caterpillars also exhibit front-to-back mimicry, brandishing hind-end filaments that resemble antennae or bearing head-like markings on their posterior ends. Although no part of a caterpillar is expendable, the hind end contains fewer nerve endings and is tougher than the all-important head. Hesitation on the part of the predator or a less-than-fatal grab at the wrong end may give the larva time to drop to the relative safety of the ground.

The best defense is often a good offense, and butterflies and caterpillars sometimes evade predators by scaring them away. Many drab butterflies have bright wing portions that they flash before closing their wings, creating a "startle" effect. Some add large eyespots to their visual assault. In a world that operates on an "eat while avoiding being eaten" premise, staring eyes spell danger. Many butterfly wings are a mosaic of false eyespots. Wood nymphs, buckeyes, American Ladies, and pearly-eyes all display false eyes that seem to belong to a much larger creature. Caterpillars also get into the act. Some eyespots are extremely convincing and three-dimensional. Others are only effective when viewed from a precise angle. But all send the menacing message, "I'm watching you—better leave me alone."

Defense tactics sometimes fall within the category of truth is stranger than fiction. The easiest way to find many blues' caterpillars is to look for attending ants. These larvae entice ant bodyguards to fend off small predators, rewarding them with sugary secretions that larvae produce within their own bodies. Pupae may continue to be guarded by attentive ants.

We have only scratched the surface of the intricacies of predator avoidance and the adaptations it engenders. Camouflage and mimicry are especially complex, not always straightforward or obvious. And a single butterfly species may simultaneously utilize a variety of protective techniques. Black Swallowtail caterpillars begin their lives as bird dropping look-a-likes (mimicry), but later develop stripes that, from a distance, allow them to blend with host plant foliage (camouflage). However, at close range, their black bands are studded with yellow spots (aposematism), creating a look distinctly reminiscent of Monarch caterpillars (mimicry). It's enough to make your head spin. Or perhaps to share with Philip Henry Gosse, "a fresh emotion of wonder and admiration."[2]

The Life Cycle

No focus on butterflies is complete without at least a cursory glance at their life cycle. A basic understanding of this process is foundational for all the species accounts that follow.

Butterflies undergo complete metamorphosis. Beginning as an egg, they pass through a distinct larval stage, then enter into a seemingly inactive state as a pupa, and finally emerge as an adult—in butterfly jargon: egg, caterpillar, chrysalid, butterfly. Each four-stage cycle comprises one generation. Some species are univoltine, completing only a single generation each year. Others are multivoltine and complete two or more full cycles annually.

Fertilized eggs contain the basic components of life. Butterfly eggs may be shaped like bullets, discs, turbans, or spheres. They range in color from pearly white to bark brown and rusty red. Many are green, but some are bright orange. The egg stage may run its course in as little as four days; however, in some species, it may last as long as ten months.

Shortly before hatching (eclosion), most eggs appear to darken as growing larvae become visible through the egg's wall. Once free of their shells, many larvae make meals of them. So many meals follow that caterpillars are often called eating machines, and they must periodically shed their skins (or cuticles) in order to accommodate their increasing mass. Whenever this saturation point is reached, larvae stop feeding and become immobile. Since the hard, inflexible head capsule is particularly limiting, a new head grows behind the old one as a new skin forms under the current cuticle. When the timing is right, the old skin splits at the head, and the caterpillar writhes, wiggles, and finally walks out of it. For a few hours, the new cuticle is very soft, allowing the caterpillar to expand to a much larger size before it hardens. The body of the caterpillar between molts is called an instar. Most species have five instars, although many lycaenids have only four, greater fritillaries have six, and metalmarks have up to nine.

Near the end of the final instar, the caterpillar prepares for the next major developmental stage. Sometimes called the pre-pupal phase, at this point, feeding ends, the gut is voided, and in some species, the larva completely changes colors. It also begins to wander in a search for the perfect pupation site—an important choice because chrysalides are immobile and unable to flee from danger. Once the selection is made, just as it does when it molts between instars, the caterpillar's cuticle splits. This time, a chrysalid wiggles out. Like all other life-cycle forms, chrysalides are diverse. Although some dangle and others lay prostrate, most are attached to a substrate. Many are hooked by their rear legs into a pad of silk, and some are also supported by a strand of silk that resembles a waist belt. For some species, the pupal phase lasts only a week, but for others, ten months pass before the final transformation occurs.

When development is almost complete, wings become visible through the semitransparent pupal covering. A short time later, the chrysalid splits, and a bedraggled butterfly struggles out. It must expand its crumpled wings and allow them to dry and harden, a process which may take several hours. Finally it flies away to begin its part in the repeating cycle.

SPECIES ACCOUNTS AND FAMILY OVERVIEWS

Using the Species Accounts

The eighty-four accounts that follow are designed to provide a glimpse of each species as we have come to know it through our years of field experience and our additional research. Although some of the information is rather technical, we have chosen to use "plain" language in these narrations so that they are accessible to those with various levels of knowledge. For this reason, we have also chosen to refer to plants and animals by their "common" or vernacular names. While there is no doubt that scientific nomenclature is the most efficient and consistent way to identify any organism, even parenthetically including these names within the accounts made them cumbersome and difficult to read. Therefore, each plant and animal mentioned by its common name within the accounts is listed with its Latin name in "Plant and Animal Associates."

With a few exceptions, we follow the Butterflies of America interactive Web site in its selection of specific butterfly names. In an effort to make this book consistent with the upcoming revision of *Wildflowers of Alabama and Adjoining States,* plant nomenclature is based on the soon-to-be published *Annotated Checklist of the Vascular Plants of Alabama.*

Sometimes we share the glimpses of others by quoting their exact words. Appropriate citations are found in the Notes.

It has never been our intent to produce a field guide—we leave that task to others; however, for the convenience of the reader, concise information, additional details that include identification tips, and range maps for each species are included in the Annotated Checklist.

Many of the photographs in this book were taken in Alabama. Sometimes, especially in the case of rare species, that was not possible. We have made every attempt to ensure that when photographed elsewhere, the butterflies, plants, and habitats are consistent with those that occur within this state.

Swallowtails
The Papilionidae

Swallowtails are attention grabbers. Large and showy, these elegant butterflies are also powerful fliers. Each of Alabama's resident species have tailed hindwings that are reminiscent of a swallow's long, forked tails—hence their familiar common name.

Swallowtail caterpillars are also famous for forked appendages. They possess deeply cleft organs called osmeteria that aid in defense against predation. Normally hidden at the back of the head, caterpillars evert and then brandish these structures when danger threatens. Osmeteria emit foul-smelling secretions composed of terpenes, primary constituents of the essential oils found within the species' host plants. Small predators are repulsed, while humans wonder, "What is that funny smell?" Long thought to be unique to the swallowtails, greater fritillary larvae also possess osmeteria, but those of the swallowtails are brighter colored and more visible.

Most swallowtail eggs are large, round, and smooth. Chrysalides resemble broken branch tips or rolled leaves, and may be brown or green, depending on both surface and season. Fall's short day lengths typically generate brown chrysalides that blend with leafless winter landscapes. Longer summer days and smooth, leafy surfaces tend to trigger green pupal color, but brown chrysalides often dangle from rough surfaces like rocks or bark, regardless of season or photoperiod.

Taxonomically, the diverse swallowtail family is divided into three subfamilies. Papilioninae, the largest, is further divided into tribes (groupings of very closely related and similar species). Swallowtails from three tribes reside in Alabama: the Aristolochia Swallowtails, the Kite Swallowtails, and the Fluted Swallowtails.

Pipevine Swallowtails belong to the tribe of Aristolochia Swallowtails, and are its only representative in Alabama. Because they are able to sequester

Basking Spicebush and Eastern Tiger swallowtails

toxic chemicals from their host plants (Aristolochias) and use them defensively against predators, many other butterflies presumably mimic them. Unlike other swallowtails in our region, Pipevines lay their eggs in small clusters, and young caterpillars feed in groups.

Zebra Swallowtails are the only Kite Swallowtails that inhabit Alabama. Typically tropical, their elongated wing shape and tube-like hindwing margins are diagnostic. Pawpaws, shrubs and trees within the Custard-Apple family, function as caterpillar food plants.

The Fluted Swallowtails encompass the majority of Alabama's swallowtail species. The name originated because male hindwing margins are lightly rolled or "fluted." Early instar caterpillars resemble bird droppings and display a white, saddle-like mark on a dark, grainy body. Within this large tribe, Black Swallowtail larvae eat plants from the Carrot/Parsley family; Giants are Citrus family feeders; Palamedes/Spicebush Swallowtails are tied to the Laurels, and the Tigers claim many families as caterpillar hosts.

Pipevine Swallowtail *Battus philenor*

Pipevine Swallowtails are poisonous, and they openly advertise it. Their black upper hindwings shimmer with metallic blue, but their undersides are emblazoned with dramatic orange spots, a classic warning or aposematic color scheme known in the natural world to signal danger. Constant fluttering, even while nectaring, draws attention to these flashing neon danger signs. Their early warning system is so effective that Pipevine Swallowtails are often considered to be the center of a mimicry ring containing at least five species of butterfly impersonators. Because the copycats are also big, black and blue, orange-spotted butterflies, they all presumably gain some protection from predation.

What makes Pipevine Swallowtails so unpalatable? The answer is contained within their larval food, a group of plants collectively known as pipe-

Pipevine Swallowtail on Common Milkweed

vines (or aristolochias). Pipevine clamors up treetops along stream and river-banks. It is covered with large, heart-shaped leaves, and odd flowers (shaped like Sherlock Holmes' pipe) dangle beneath its foliage. Virginia-Snakeroot, another aristolochia, is a small, upright plant that grows sporadically in open woodlands. Both pipevine species contain aristocholic acids and car-diac glycosides, phytochemicals that render them distasteful and harmful to vertebrate predators. Pipevine Swallowtail caterpillars bypass toxic ef-fects by sequestering molecules within their bodies. They keep these poison pouches throughout metamorphosis and into adulthood, passing deleteri-ous effects to any predator inexperienced enough to ingest them.Like their parents, caterpillars employ aposematic warning coloration. Brown or black bodies are covered with two rows of short orange tubercles. Fleshy filaments complete the look. Bypassing typical swallowtail mimicry and camouflage techniques, their early instars do not resemble bird droppings. Emerging

Early instar caterpillars (red form) congregating on Pipevine

Pipevine
Swallowtail
egg cluster

from small groups of dark orange eggs, caterpillars initially feed in groups, perhaps maximizing the visibility of their warning signals. Those feeding on pipevines generally have ample food supplies, but Virginia-Snakeroot eaters must scour the woodland floor for additional plants in order to satiate voracious appetites and complete larval development. Chrysalides occur in two color forms and are the only camouflaged life-cycle stage. Brown pupae resemble broken twigs or withered leaves while green chrysalides look like furled foliage.

Warning colors aside, early field guides referred to these butterflies as Blue Swallowtails for good reason. Their iridescent blue hindwings glisten and glimmer as they catch sunlight at different angles. In a world of butterfly mimics, Pipevine Swallowtails are beautiful—but dangerous—originals.

Opposite: Final instar Pipevine Swallowtail caterpillar (black form) on Pipevine

Brown Pipevine Swallowtail chrysalid camouflaged with bark

Pipevine Swallowtail displaying its iridescent wings

Zebra Swallowtail *Eurytides marcellus*

A large, black-and-white-striped butterfly flying in Alabama *is* a Zebra Swallowtail. Long-tailed and unmistakable, it flies in early spring, followed by a longer tailed summer generation. In good years, a third, extremely long-tailed brood is the seasons' finale.

Their tails may be long, but Zebra Swallowtails' proboscises are unusually short, limiting nectar sources to short-tubed flowers such as flowering plums and blackberries. Slender striped wings are adapted for both maneuverability and camouflage, allowing Zebra Swallowtails to flutter and swoop through woodland understories. Visually, their telltale stripes make them difficult to follow as they glide through dappled sunlight and shadows.

Look for Zebra Swallowtails near pawpaws, their only caterpillar food. In most of Alabama, there are two species: Common Pawpaw and Small-Fruit Pawpaw. Common Pawpaws are trees that grow near creeks and rivers and in floodplains. Large leaved and tropical in appearance, they bear meaty fruits that inspired "sweet little Susie to pick 'em up and put 'em in her pocket."

Left: Caterpillar (green form) on Small-Fruit Pawpaw

Opposite: Zebra Swallowtail (long-tailed summer form) on Fringed Bluestars

Above: Zebra Swallowtail
caterpillar (dark form) on
Common Pawpaw

Left: Zebra Swallowtail
chrysalid on Common
Pawpaw

Small-Fruit Pawpaws inhabit drier, open woods. As their name implies, foliage, flowers, and fruits are small in scale and can be easily overlooked in woodland vegetation.

Zebra Swallowtails are skilled pawpaw detectors and deposit globe-shaped eggs on twigs, flower buds, and velvety new leaves. Newly hatched caterpillars appear to be solid black specks, but after molting, they display camouflaging stripes. Enlarged thoracic segments create a curious hump-backed appearance, which exaggerates if danger is detected. When alarmed, caterpillars quickly extrude bright yellow osmeteria, blasting out foul-smelling chemicals derived from acetogenins, insecticidal pawpaw chemicals. Fifth instar caterpillars transform into short, stout chrysalides that are "shaped almost like the body of a pig," according to Philip Henry Gosse.[1] Leafy green or bark brown, they are often attached to their pawpaw hosts.

Zebras belong to the worldwide group of Kite Swallowtails, a tropical genus named for its wing shape. They are the sole members that have adapted to our North American, less-than-tropical climate. Fortunately for Alabamians, Zebra Swallowtails are at home in our state wherever pawpaws abound.

Zebra Swallowtail (short-tailed spring form) on a flowering plum

Black Swallowtail *Papilio polyxenes*

Black Swallowtails are at home in gardens throughout Alabama. Drawn by showy, fragrant flowers, they linger in herb and vegetable gardens that include plants in the Carrot/Parsley family, their caterpillar hosts. Cultivated species include parsley, dill, fennel, and caraway. But Black Swallowtails range far beyond the garden. Meadows, prairies, wetlands, and woodland edges that support native carrots such as Hairy Angelica, mock bishopweeds, and naturalized Queen Anne's Lace are also prime Black Swallowtail habitat.

Gardeners who never noticed Black Swallowtail butterflies will be familiar with their striking green-and-black-striped caterpillars. Sometimes called parsley worms, they begin life as brown-and-white bird-dropping mimics but quickly transform into lean, green, eating machines. They devour entire plants, despite the fact that carrot family members are loaded with furanocoumarins, toxic chemicals which interfere with DNA processing. Black Swal-

Above: Caterpillar eating
Hairy Angelica

Left: Early instar caterpillar
resting on Common Golden
Zizia

Opposite: Black Swallowtail
nectaring on a native azalea

Black Swallowtail caterpillar extruding osmeteria while clinging to dill

lowtails ingest large doses, rendering themselves mildly distasteful to hungry predators. Caterpillars do not wait to be tasted, but also engage in a "prevent defense." When danger is detected, they quickly puff up, rear back, and eject bright orange osmeteria from their heads. These organs spray foul-smelling bucolic acid at attackers. If defensive tactics are successful and caterpillars reach maturity, they form either brown or green chrysalides, depending on season and surface texture.

Butterflies retain some toxicity from caterpillar days and maximize this advantage by mimicking more highly poisonous Pipevine Swallowtails. Females are better impersonators. Their dorsal (upper surface) wings are close copies of Pipevine's solid black surface, clouded with shimmery blue. Male butterflies display bright yellow bands and only minimal blue scaling. Like their Pipevine Swallowtail model, both sexes display prominent orange spots on ventral (under surface) hindwings, advertising their bad taste with warning coloration and further confusing predators as to their true identity.

Black Swallowtail chrysalid attached to Hairy Angelica

Male Black Swallowtail on a native azalea

Female Black Swallowtail on a native azalea

Giant Swallowtail *Papilio cresphontes*

Giant Swallowtails seem larger than life. With five-inch wingspans, they are not necessarily Alabama's biggest butterflies (female tiger swallowtails claim that distinction), but in the words of Philip Henry Gosse, they have "a magnificent appearance." Viewed from above, chocolate-brown butterflies are festooned with crisscrossed yellow bands. Seen from below, the color scheme is reversed: creamy yellow butterflies are delicately outlined and etched in blackest brown. Flapping wings create a gentle strobe effect, and as Gosse noted, "the contrast between prevailing colours of the upper and under surface is very observable as the insect floats carelessly along."[2]

Giant Swallowtail caterpillars are magnificent in their own right. Like most swallowtails, earliest instars resemble bird droppings, but unlike the others, Giants never completely discard that disguise. Fully mature larvae present an impressive, if disgusting, countenance. Their mottled brown color pattern

Giant Swallowtail on Wild Blue Phlox

serves them well. In addition to creating the dung disguise, it also enables larger caterpillars to rest on similarly patterned tree bark, blending invisibly into that background. Gosse compared the color combination to a piebald horse, but it also brings to mind a small, scaly brown snake, perhaps discouraging meal-seeking predators. The frightening effect is accentuated when defensive caterpillars display bright red osmeterial glands, eerily reminiscent of a viper's forked tongue.

Caterpillar camouflaged with Hoptree bark

Above: A defensive Giant Swallowtail caterpillar tucking its head to present a false face

Left: Giant Swallowtail osmeteria

Their appetite for cultivated citrus plants is infamous, and Florida's commercial growers curse Giant Swallowtail caterpillars as "Orange Dogs" that damage their cash crops. In Alabama, larvae must rely on little-known Citrus family members for nourishment. Although herb gardeners may find them eating Common Rue, Giant Swallowtail populations depend on native citruses like Hoptree and Southern Prickly-Ash. Superficially, these small trees

Giant Swallowtail caterpillar with Hoptree samaras

bear little resemblance to their culinary cousins. Rather than tart, round fruits, Hoptree produces dry, papery-thin, one-seeded fruits called samaras, and Southern Prickly-Ash bears clusters of husk-covered capsules that open to reveal dark, round seeds. Yet they contain the same ethereal oils responsible for typical citrus aromas, as well as the family's bitter-tasting triteripenes, alkaloids, and calcium oxalate crystals, all chemical deterrents to hungry herbivores.

Giant Swallowtails emerge from crusty chrysalides that look like broken branches. They avidly nectar at many different flowers, their constantly fluttering wings blurring their two-toned color scheme. Nonetheless, their appearance is undeniably magnificent.

Above: Giant Swallowtail nectaring on Wild Bergamot

Opposite: Giant Swallowtail chrysalid

Appalachian Tiger Swallowtail *Papilio appalachiensis*

Who would have guessed that hidden within one of America's most widely known and recognizable butterfly species was another similar but separate entity? Lepidopterists had long scratched their heads over unusually large, strangely shaped tiger swallowtails that seemed to fly only in the mountains, but it was not until 2002 that Harry Pavulaan and David Wright described and named a new species, Appalachian Tiger Swallowtail.

At first glance, "Appys," as they are often called, seem virtually identical to Eastern Tiger Swallowtails, but there are relevant and discernable differences in appearance, life history, and range. Appalachian Tigers are as much as 20 percent larger than first-generation Eastern Tigers, a size difference that is particularly noticeable when both species are seen puddling or nectaring side by side. Wing shape also differs. Appalachian hindwings are triangular rather than rounded, and edges appear stair-stepped rather than scalloped. While Eastern Tigers have multiple broods that stretch across temperate months,

Appalachian Tiger Swallowtail basking on Mountain-Laurel

Appys are univoltine, flying only in spring and possibly into early summer, roughly between Eastern Tigers' first two generations.

Appalachian Tiger Swallowtails avidly seek flower nectar, and males frequently congregate in large puddle clubs in their search for minerals. Unfortunately, females are wary and reclusive, so details regarding reproductive behavior have been slow in coming. Currently, only Black Cherry is a confirmed host plant, but additional hosts are suspected. Range is limited to the Appalachian Mountains, where Appys are seasonally abundant, and at times, the most prevalent tiger swallowtail in the area.

In May 2008, Appalachian Tiger Swallowtails were officially documented in Alabama's own Appalachian foothills when we found them (nectaring on blackberry blossoms) in the mountains of northeast Jackson County. Many exciting discoveries remain in order to determine distribution, host plant preference, and complete life-cycle details, not only within our state, but throughout their range. Citizen scientists can play a valuable role in putting together the pieces of Appalachian Tiger Swallowtails' life-history puzzle.

Appalachian Tiger Swallowtail nectaring on blackberry blossoms

Eastern Tiger Swallowtail *Papilio glaucus*

Eastern Tiger Swallowtails are a study in stripes. Upper wings, lower wings, topsides, bottom sides, and even bodies are marked. Jagged black bars contrast sharply with bright yellow wings, but this striking combination allows tiger swallowtails to disappear in the canopy just as striped Bengal Tigers blend with Asian savannas. Blue hindwing frosting softens the striated effect, with females displaying more extensive blue scaling than males. Despite their protective color pattern, many female tigers have shifted from camouflage to mimicry to avoid predation. In Alabama, where Pipevine Swallowtails are common, most Eastern Tiger females are predominately black rather than yellow, and they easily pass for their poisonous relatives. But just as the pro-

Above: Eastern Tiger Swallowtail (male) on a wild plum

Opposite: Eastern Tiger Swallowtail (dark female) on Bear's-Foot

Eastern Tiger Swallowtail (yellow female) on Bear's-Foot

verbial tiger cannot change its stripes, a close look at all of these dusky females reveals that black zigzags still bolt across their wings, appearing as
shadows against a dark background. Sometimes butterflies even display a
mixture of light and dark color forms, and yellow wings may be heavily pep-
pered with black.

Caterpillars commonly eat young Tulip-Poplar, Black Cherry, or Sweet-Bay
Magnolia leaves, although Eastern Tigers have a relatively generalized palate.
Their larval food plants are more diverse than any other swallowtail species,
and as many as thirteen plant families are represented in their host plant rep-

Above: Eastern Tiger Swallowtail
(intermediate form) on a wild plum

Left: Eastern Tiger Swallowtail egg

ertoire. This unusual adaptability results from their ability to produce special enzymes that neutralize a wide variety of chemical plant defenses.

Female Eastern Tigers deposit pearly green eggs on host plant foliage. Newly emerged caterpillars look like brown-and-white bird droppings, but older larvae shift pretenses and resemble tiny green snakes. Peering from leaf troughs constructed by pulling edges together with silk, their false eye markings are small and beady. If attacked, caterpillars counter by projecting yellow, Y-shaped osmeteria, which emit noxious, smelly chemicals. When pupation time approaches, leafy green larvae make a final color change.

Left: Early instar Eastern Tiger Swallowtail caterpillar resting on its webbing

Below: Late instar Eastern Tiger Swallowtail caterpillar extruding osmeteria

They once again turn brown before metamorphosing into bark-colored chrysalides.

Two, sometimes three, generations of Eastern Tiger Swallowtails span spring, summer, and fall. Early season tigers avidly nectar at native azalea and wild plum blossoms. Later broods produce larger butterflies that count thistles and ironweed among their favorite flowers. In addition to their role as nectar drinkers, males are also enthusiastic, gregarious "puddlers," and their gatherings are common sights along riverbanks and rural roads.

In 1989 the exquisitely striped Eastern Tiger Swallowtail, gloriously beautiful, widespread, and well known, was adopted by the state legislature as Alabama's official butterfly.

Pre-pupal phase
Eastern Tiger
Swallowtail
caterpillar
exhibiting
color change

Left: Eastern Tiger Swallowtail chrysalid

Below: Eastern Tiger Swallowtail (male) on Bear's-Foot

Eastern Tiger Swallowtail (female) on a wild plum

Spicebush Swallowtail *Papilio troilus*

Spicebush Swallowtails add a splash of green to Alabama's swallowtail color palette. Once known as Green-Clouded Swallowtails, males of the species were aptly named. Expanses of blue-green scales drift across their black hindwings, and green chevrons outline lower wing edges. Females are another story. They also sport green chevrons, but their hindwing clouds are decidedly blue, making them excellent mimics of their poisonous relative, the Pipevine Swallowtail. This marked resemblance presumably gains protection from predators who avoid distasteful encounters with large black-and-blue butterflies.

Above: Spicebush Swallowtail (female) on Trumpet-Weed

Opposite: Spicebush Swallowtail (male) on a native azalea

Above left: Early instar Spicebush Swallowtail caterpillar on Northern Spicebush

Above right: Late instar Spicebush Swallowtail caterpillar on Northern Spicebush

Opposite: Spicebush Swallowtail caterpillar exhibiting its prepupal color change

Like their mothers, Spicebush Swallowtail caterpillars are consummate copycats and constantly change color and form. First instar caterpillars are disguised as bird droppings, but they quickly discard that look in favor of dramatic false eyes, virtually guaranteed to convince predators they have encountered a small snake or distasteful tree frog. As larvae grow and shed their skins (or cuticles), they are first brown, then green, and finally, as they prepare for pupation, a startling banana yellow.

Spicebush Swallowtail caterpillars are engineers as well as imitators. Very

young larvae construct protective shelters by chewing small flaps into leaves, which they bend and secure over themselves. Older caterpillars fold leaves in half and lay down a pad of silk. Drying threads shrink, causing leaves to curl into tubes. When not eating, the small architect rests inside, only its goggle-eyed false face visible from the opening.

Caterpillars and butterflies are found near the edges of fields and wood-lands that support their primary host plants, spicebushes and Sassafras. All are members of the aromatic Laurel family, and both are known for their distinctive fragrances. Northern Spicebush is a spreading shrub that inhabits rich, fertile woodlands. Crushing its leaves or stems releases a spicy lemon scent. Sassafras is a medium-sized, root-beer-scented tree known for its use in file powder and spring tonic tea. It bears leaves in three different shapes—oval, three lobed, and mitten shaped—any of which might shelter and feed a growing caterpillar.

Spicebush Swallowtails are avid nectarers, their long proboscises reaching deep into floral tubes of plants that include native azaleas, honeysuckles, and milkweeds. In nineteenth-century Alabama, Philip Henry Gosse noticed them nectaring in his "nice little prairie knoll," and he quickly became enamored. After discussing other "gorgeous swallowtails," he concluded that Green-Clouded Swallowtail was "a more beautiful species than all of these."[3]

Spicebush Swallowtail caterpillar's
sheltering leaf "flap"

Left: Spicebush Swallowtail caterpillar's rolled leaf shelter

Below: A nectaring Spicebush Swallowtail

Palamedes Swallowtail *Papilio palamedes*

Palamedes Swallowtails are known as swamp butterflies—the signature species of southern wetlands. But Palamedes Swallowtails are more accurately described as Redbay Butterflies, for they can be expected wherever redbays flourish. While Swamp Redbay is solely resident in swamps, bays, and marsh edges, redbay also grows in drier, coastal plain woodlands, allowing Palamedes Swallowtails to fly beyond the wetlands.

Large, dark Palamedes Swallowtails are steady and graceful in flight, never fluttery. Closely related to Spicebush Swallowtails, family resemblance is strongest in larval stages. Both species begin life in typical swallowtail bird-dung disguises, both morph into small snake or tree frog look-alikes, and both turn a bright banana yellow before forming their chrysalides.

Palamedes Swallowtail on a blazing-star

Early instar caterpillar resting in leaf shelter on a partially eaten redbay leaf

Late instar caterpillar in redbay leaf shelter

At first glance, the caterpillar cousins appear to be identical twins, but early instar Palamedes' posterior ends are solid white, while Spicebush larval "tails" combine brown with white. And while Spicebush cats are flap-folding leaf rollers, Palamedes are apt to rest totally exposed on upper leaf surfaces. This behavior is not as risky as it seems, because redbay leaves are almost always deformed and disfigured by Redbay Psyllid larvae, tiny nymphs whose saliva causes leaf margins to swell and curl into popcorn-like galls. Harmless

Left: Palamedes Swallowtail chrysalid on redbay

Below: Palamedes Swallowtail caterpillar silked into position for transition to chrysalid

to plants, these two-toned, bumpy formations coincidentally provide additional protective camouflage for two-toned, bumpy Palamedes caterpillars.

In spite of remarkable adaptations that evolved over thousands of years, Palamedes Swallowtails are faced with a fast-moving, immediate threat to their existence. Redbays are succumbing by the thousands to a vascular wilt pathogen in the same genus as the tree-killing Dutch elm disease. Carried by the Redbay Ambrosia Beetle, which was introduced from Southeast Asia into the United States near Savannah, Georgia, in 2002, it is moving south at a rate of twenty miles per year. At the time of this writing, it has not yet reached Alabama.

According to the University of Georgia tree expert Kim Coder, "Redbay is a biological, ecological, and cultural treasure of the deep woods."[4] So is Palamedes Swallowtail, the Redbay Butterfly.

Palamedes Swallowtail on a blazing-star

Sulphurs and Whites
The Pieridae

Sulphurs and whites are among Alabama's most abundant and conspicuous butterflies. Collectively called pierids, with few exceptions, they are sun-loving nectar drinkers that coexist with people in gardens or other agricultural settings.

Pierids share a color palette of white, yellow, and orange and are trimmed or marked with black. Their wing colors (pteridines) are derived from uric acid, a waste product, stored from caterpillar days. Pteridine pigments either reflect or absorb ultraviolet light, creating distinctive wing patterns that are invisible to human eyes. Because some pierid species look remarkably similar, these fluorescences are extremely important for potential mate recognition. In addition to sexual differences (dimorphism), seasonal color forms also exist. As a rule, short days produce smaller, darker individuals that are better able to absorb heat in cool seasons, while spring and summer butterflies are larger, lighter, and more heat tolerant.

Eggs are brightly colored spikes, first white, often turning either yellow or orange. Caterpillars are wormlike and highly camouflaged. Countershading and striping enhance their basic green color scheme. Chrysalides strongly resemble furled leaves, and many are distinctly pointed. Although a few pierids are univoltine, most are multibrooded. The pierids are divided into two major subfamilies: the Sulphurs and the Whites.

The Sulphurs are bright yellow and/or orange butterflies, although females sometimes assume white or "alba" forms. Many sulphur caterpillars eat legumes from the diverse Pea/Bean family. These plants are nitrogen-rich and capable of producing rapid growth, but they are nontoxic and provide little if any chemical protection for those who eat them.

Snowy wing pigments give the Whites an obvious name. Their caterpillars typically eat mustards, and although other plants occasionally fit the bill, all

Southern Dogface on Brazilian Vervain

contain glucosinolates, bitter mustard oil molecules that may render their partakers at least somewhat unpalatable.

Like their host plants, pierids are far ranging and may be found from coastal beaches to mountain summits. Although a few are homebodies (notably West Virginia White), many move from host plant to host plant, colonizing new territories as they go. Collectively, sulphurs and whites often emigrate to northern climates during summer months, only to retrace their steps as winter approaches.

Barred Yellow *Eurema daira*

Tiny Barred Yellows are permanent residents of south Alabama, but in autumn, they may pop up anywhere in the state. These vagrants are found in pinewoods, sandhills, roadsides, and other sunny areas that support their easily overlooked, Pea family host plants. Newly colonized Barred Yellow territories are often short-lived, because freezing temperatures leave only permanent populations intact. In those warm areas, adult Barred Yellows are veritable butterfly Methuselahs, living four to five months in reproductive diapause. When spring returns, reproduction begins, and many generations follow.

Barred Yellows maintain their constantly changing lifestyle by assuming many adaptive forms. Summer/wet season butterflies are paler and smaller than their late-season counterparts. Winter/dry season individuals display brick-red wings that blend with fallen leaves and also absorb heat, aiding in thermoregulation. In addition to seasonal variations, male and female butterflies also differ in outward appearance. Males are distinctly barred: their upper forewings display a heavy, black, horizontal line that looks drawn by a Magic Marker. These namesake bars are often visible in flight and may

Barred Yellow (lighter summer form) on beggarticks

sometimes be seen through closed wings, but they are most apparent during courtship. In a bizarre display of machismo, an amorous male sidles up to his potential partner and waves one thickly lined, disjointed forewing in her face while releasing sex-inducing pheromones. If she is previously unmated and sufficiently impressed, mating occurs. Female wing bars are faint, and winter individuals may lack them altogether. Barred Yellows exhibit so many different markings and color forms that the respected lepidopterist-author Rick Cech suggests "Variable Sulphur" as a more appropriate name.[5]

Left: Courtship display

Below: Barred Yellow (darker winter form)

Barred Yellows typically lay their eggs on weedy joint-vetches and pencil-flowers where small green caterpillars eat new growth. Many joint-vetches are introduced weeds, but American Joint-Vetch is a southeastern native. A reseeding summer annual, it is often planted as wildlife food and also as a nitrogen-fixing cover crop. Side-Beak Pencil-Flower is a common, if seldom noticed, tiny leaved, sprawling native perennial that grows in many habitats and bears egg-yolk yellow, pea-type blossoms. These legumes and their close relatives inhabit so many ecosystems throughout the state that passing Barred Yellows are seldom far from suitable host plants during their late-summer travels.

Barred Yellow caterpillar on Side-Beak Pencil-Flower

Left: Barred Yellow chrysalid

Below: Barred Yellow on a frogfruit

Sleepy Orange *Eurema nicippe*

Anyone who has ever watched a Sleepy Orange zip through a field or dart across a road knows there is nothing "sleepy" about its behavior. It is a relief to learn that the name's origin derives not from *flight* patterns but from *wing* patterns. Small black crescents, reminiscent of closed or sleeping eyes, mark the forewing. "Rambling Orange" has been proposed as a more logical name since, like all sulphurs, Sleepy Oranges seldom hold their wings where any "sleepy" field marks are visible.

Whatever their name, these midsized orange butterflies abound in sunny areas throughout the state. Although they may not always survive north Alabama's freezing winters, they quickly recolonize in spring. In that season of the year, they are often seen flying in woodlands, perhaps because their more typical, open-field habitats are later to sprout new growth. By midsummer and fall, they behave like a different species and fly by the dozens around cultivated fields. Adults avidly nectar at many types of flowers, and males are common sights at puddle clubs.

Sleepy Orange caterpillars eat leguminous plants known as sennas and partridge-peas. Both are common across the state, where alien sennas invade agricultural fields, and partridge-peas are planted as erosion control agents on roadsides and bobwhite quail bait on hunting grounds. Sleepy Oranges dot host leaves with slender eggs, and emergent caterpillars eat both foliage and flowers. Green, wormlike larvae are densely covered with minuscule hairs, giving them a velveteen appearance. Camouflage is a primary defense against predators. Partridge-pea green in color, they are also lighter on top than bottom, an optical illusion called countershading, which reduces conspicuous shadows cast on upper body surfaces.

Several Sleepy Orange generations are produced each year, and flight continues into December. Late-season butterflies emerge washed in brick orange, perhaps helping them blend with fallen leaves. Those that survive winter freezes do so in reproductive diapause, another adaptation to conserve precious energy and maximize chances for survival until warm weather returns.

Sleepy Orange on Blue Mistflower

Sleepy Orange displaying namesake "sleepy eye" marks

Sleepy Orange caterpillar on Common Partridge-Pea

Sleepy Orange (summer form)

Sleepy Orange (winter form)

Little Yellow *Pyrisitia lisa*

These charming little butterflies are the most widespread and common of Alabama's small sulphurs. Living year-round in frost-free areas, as soon as temperatures allow, Little Yellows quickly fill gaps caused by winter's cold. Although petite in size, they push farther north than any of their close relatives, and they are capable of huge southbound fall migrations.

"Little Yellow" is a descriptive name—most of the time. Sexes are dimorphic, with males typically brighter and more solidly marked, and (like many other sulphurs), females are sometimes white rather than yellow. Males are not confused, for they locate potential mates with ultraviolet vision, utilizing its additional cues and patterns for recognition. They bear special pheromone-producing scent scales called androconia, located near their bodies on the forewings' underside. In order for females to become sexually receptive, they must first be showered with the males' enticing perfume. Uninterested females flutter wildly or fly straight up in the air.

Little Yellow (male) on Common Partridge-Pea

Little Yellows are residents of fields, roadsides, and sunny edges where they lay their eggs on legumes. New growth attracts females that deposit cylindrical, pale yellow eggs on young foliage tips. Hosts include partridge-peas, sensitive-briers, and puffs, all producing finely divided compound leaves that are perfect for camouflaging Little Yellow's slender green caterpillars. Several have touch-sensitive leaflets that close on contact, further concealing little leaf eaters. Partridge-peas are also common hosts for Cloudless Sulphurs, but competition is minimized since their caterpillars prefer to eat flowers and seedpods, while Little Yellow larvae choose leaves. Chrysalides are often attached to host plant stems and are as pea green as their caterpillar predecessors. No cryptic brown camouflage is required, since Little Yellows do not overwinter in their pupal stage, but spend cold months in reproductive diapause as adults.

Little Yellows fly low to the ground and drink nectar from many low-growing flowers. In addition, males avidly sip minerals from damp earth. Their small forms are common constituents of late-summer puddle clubs.

Little Yellow (female) on Maryland Golden-Aster

Little Yellow caterpillar on a puff

Praying Mantis eyeing Little Yellow puddle club

Little Yellow chrysalid on Common Partridge-Pea

Clouded Sulphur *Colias philodice*

When identifying Clouded Sulphurs, think lemon yellow. They are easily confused with their close relatives, Orange Sulphurs, but Cloudeds never display a hint of orange or gold. Although both species occasionally fly together in weedy or agricultural fields, Clouded Sulphurs are seldom seen in Alabama. Originally a more northern species, they moved south in the early 1900s as more western-based Orange Sulphurs moved east. In the resulting mixture, Cloudeds took a backseat to Orange Sulphurs, which are now much more abundant.

Identification problems are intensified by frequently occurring white ("alba") females. Almost one-third of Clouded Sulphur females are white, an adaptation that allows them to divert nitrogen away from yellow pigment production into more efficient egg production. Since Orange Sulphurs share this adaptive trait, white females are virtually indistinguishable in the field. Paradoxically, look-alike females have no problem in recognizing males of their own species. Ultraviolet (UV) coloration, invisible under normal light to human eyes, adds another dimension to butterfly vision. Clouded Sulphur males absorb UV light while Orange Sulphur males reflect it, so in the eyes of the opposite sex, they look as different as night and day.

Correctly identifying caterpillars is also difficult—Clouded and Orange sulphur larvae look exactly alike. Both share a taste for clovers and other legumes, and both are well-camouflaged night eaters. Clouded caterpillars remain true to their northern heritage and thrive in slightly lower temperatures, allowing them to more quickly complete development in cool weather.

Clouded Sulphurs are most likely to occur in north Alabama, although they may expand south in favorable years. Look for them in more natural, less agricultural habitats than Orange Sulphurs typically occupy. And keep in mind that when a medium-sized yellow sulphur takes flight, even a hint of orange means it is *not* a Clouded Sulphur.

Clouded Sulphur on an aster

Caterpillar on Yellow Sweet-Clover

Clouded Sulphur ("alba" form) on Eastern Purple-Coneflower

Orange Sulphur *Colias eurythema*

Orange Sulphurs are not always orange. Despite their label, they display varying amounts of their namesake color, and some lack it altogether. Springtime females are often white, while summer males display more orange than those of earlier broods. So many variations in shading and hue exist that over the years nearly a dozen species names have been assigned to Orange Sulphurs' various guises, all of which are now recognized as one single, but highly inconsistent species.

Once called the Alfalfa Butterfly, Orange Sulphurs' primary populations were based in the western United Sates, where their host plant of choice was (predictably) alfalfa. As eastern forests were cleared and converted to farms and pastures, Alfalfa butterflies followed alfalfa's eastward march, reaching Alabama in the 1930s. By the 1950s, the state's alfalfa crops were declining due to weevil infestations, but Orange Sulphurs were here to stay, having discovered a treasure trove of other acceptable legumes. Today, ubiquitous clovers and vetches satisfy larval nutritional needs and serve as primary host plants.

Orange Sulphur nectaring on Stiff Tickseed

Orange Sulphur ("alba" form) on a vetch

Orange Sulphur ("rosa" form) on Red Clover

Legumes are nitrogen rich and highly nutritious but typically lack protective chemical compounds. To compensate, Orange Sulphur caterpillars rely on cryptic coloration to avoid hungry meal seekers. They blend seamlessly with green stems and leaves and make themselves even more inconspicuous by eating at night. Rapid development and overlapping broods ensure that many generations are produced each year.

Orange Sulphurs are quintessential butterflies: sun-seeking, nectar-drinking, habitat generalists. They flutter through fields and meadows, pastures and farms, gardens and roadsides where they pause to sip at a succession of flowers that range from dandelions in the spring to asters in the fall. These avid puddlers are familiar sights along rural roads. In spite of changing land use and the conversion of farmland to urban development, Orange Sulphurs seem to have it made. Nonnative legumes in the southern landscape continue to increase as do Orange Sulphur larvae. Even global warming may benefit this highly adaptable butterfly, enabling it to extend its northernmost winter range.

Orange Sulphur caterpillar on Crimson Clover

Male and female Orange
Sulphurs exhibiting courtship behaviors

Southern Dogface *Zerene cesonia*

Some say the dog's face is schnauzer-like. Others think it looks like a poodle. Most are lucky to see it at all, because, like typical sulphurs, Southern Dog-faces rarely hold their wings open for a good look at their name-inspiring black markings. The best views most of us get of their dog-faced upper surfaces are quick, in-flight peeks or backlit, closed wing glimpses.

Southern Dogfaces are a hit-or-miss proposition throughout much of their range. Known as migrants, they often merely wander through areas, showing up sporadically from year to year. But in Alabama and Mississippi's blackland prairies, they are reliably resident and at times, the prairies' most common butterfly. What keeps these bright yellow pierids on the prairies? One answer is certainly their high concentrations of prairie-clovers (or daleas), favored caterpillar food plants. Two species commonly occur: one is purple and the other, white. Both bear cone-headed flowers wreathed with tiny blossoms,

Southern Dogface on Azure Blue Sage

Southern Dogface ("rosa" form) on Stiff Tickseed

Southern Dogface revealing its dogface wing pattern while in flight

and both produce pinnately compound leaves (Purple Prairie-Clover's are more finely cut and needle-like than those of White Prairie-Clover). Female dogfaces use both clovers interchangeably and deposit their white, spindly eggs on first one, then the other. Prairies are not the only rare environments that support daleas and dogfaces. Gattinger's Prairie-Clover is common in north Alabama's rare cedar grove glades, additional strongholds for Southern Dogface butterflies.

In spite of their affinity for rare and unusual habitats, Southern Dogfaces are renowned travelers, often encountered en route to new locations. Another favorite host plant, False Indigo, helps them on their way. A tall, purple-flowered shrub with typical Pea family foliage, it grows along riverbanks and waterways—perfect routes for migrational movements.

Southern Dogface females deposit single, spike-shaped eggs on their leguminous hosts. Caterpillars eat nitrogen-rich leaves, resting on midribs in early instars and on stems when they are larger. Although basically leafy green, some are countershaded with a single horizontal line, while others are also encircled with yellow and black vertical stripes. Chrysalides are dangling leaf-like structures, remarkable only when butterfly emergence is imminent. Then a dog's face is clearly visible, providing the best look at an otherwise elusive field mark.

Southern Dogface
egg on a prairie-clover

Southern Dogface green caterpillar on False Indigo

Above: A male Southern Dogface waiting for a female to emerge from chrysalid

Left: Immediately prior to emergence, a dog-faced wing is visible in this Southern Dogface chrysalid

Opposite: Striped Southern Dogface caterpillar on Purple Prairie-Clover

Cloudless Sulphur *Phoebis sennae*

Cloudless Sulphurs are Alabama's most widespread and common yellow butterflies. They fly from border to border throughout spring and summer months, and autumn populations rise to astonishing numbers as northern migrants join local residents. During fall, southbound individuals are common sights along interstates and other roadways, covering as many as twelve miles per day. Millions of these powerful fliers head toward central and south Florida to avoid winter freezes.

In addition to strong wings and excellent sun compasses, Cloudless Sulphurs are equipped with exceptionally long proboscises. They routinely drink from honeysuckles, native azaleas, and lobelias—flowers typically reserved

Cloudless Sulphur (male)
on Cardinal-Flower

Left: Cloudless Sulphur (female) on Savannah Hibiscus

Below: Cloudless Sulphurs have unusually long proboscises

for hummingbird bills. Cloudless Sulphurs, Cardinal-Flowers, and a clear blue sky are an electrifying sight.

Breeding grounds are sunny areas where senna plants are found. Whether alien or native, sennas are nitrogen-rich legumes with pinnately compound leaves, and often occur in human-impacted sites such as agricultural field edges, roadways, and power cuts. Common Partridge-Pea is a Cloudless Sulphur favorite, and its common use as both bobwhite quail attractant and highway erosion control agent has been a boon for sulphur butterflies. Throughout most of Alabama, butterfly gardeners who grow Common Partridge-Pea will certainly play host to Cloudless Sulphur caterpillars.

Female Cloudless Sulphurs deposit eggs singly on senna leaves, where ova quickly turn from creamy white to orange. Caterpillars will eat foliage but prefer a diet of flowers and seedpods. Reminiscent of the old adage, "You are what you eat," larvae that primarily eat flowers are yellow, while leaf eaters tend to be green. They are marked with assorted patterns of solids, stripes, and dots, but each form is highly camouflaged, whether on flowers, stems, or leaves.

Cloudless Sulphur caterpillar on a senna

Cloudless Sulphur
caterpillars
exhibiting many
color forms as
they eat Common
Partridge-Pea

Because of their high nitrogen content, sennas promote quick larval growth, but they do not transfer chemical protection to their consumers since they themselves are not toxic. In their defense against herbivores, partridge-peas contain special glands called extrafloral nectaries that secrete sweet liquid to entice ants to their stems. Lured by their sugary treats, predatory ants also make quick work of soft-bodied leaf eaters like Cloudless Sulphur caterpillars. Final instar survivors form lovely, leaf-like chrysalides that recline from host stems or nearby structures. Like their larval predecessors, pupae come in several colors and patterns, including a striking rosy form.

Cloudless Sulphur chrysalid on Common Partridge-Pea

Cloudless Sulphur chrysalid ("rosa" form)

Falcate Orangetip *Anthocharis midea*

Falcate Orangetips punctuate spring's woodlands with tiny flashes of color. Only male wings are tipped with orange, producing a strobe effect as they constantly patrol paths in search of plainer, black and white females. Butterfly enthusiasts can easily recognize both sexes by their small size and telltale hooked or "falcate" forewings. Their white under surfaces are heavily marbled with charcoal, allowing the miniature "flashers" and "flashees" to disappear among leaf litter, rocks, and twigs as they huddle with closed wings during cool spells.

Falcate Orangetips fly only in spring and, like most pierids, their single caterpillar brood uses mustard plants for its larval food. From tiny, transient weeds to fleeting spring wildflowers, woodland cresses and toothworts are common orangetip hosts. Close examination often reveals vivid orange, spindle-shaped eggs on flowers or along stems—typically only one egg per

Falcate Orangetip (male) on Yellow False Garlic

plant. A female orangetip quickly notices previously placed, brightly colored ova and searches for an unused plant on which to deposit her next potential offspring. Because of their mother's careful choices, emergent crawlers face little competition for limited food supplies, and, since this species is noted for its caterpillar cannibalism, predation by siblings is also eliminated. Colorfully striped caterpillars primarily eat protein-rich flowers and immature seeds, so growth is rapid. Larval development is often complete in ten days, but the pupal stage lasts ten months, so chrysalid design and placement is crucial. In an amazing adaptation, a final-instar caterpillar attaches itself to a twig or branch, completes its final molt, and exposes a chrysalid shaped exactly like a painfully sharp thorn. Prowling predators discover a structure that looks more likely to impale them than provide a crunchy snack.

When adult Falcate Orangetips emerge in early spring, they retain some of their host plants' distasteful mustard oils, and are at least somewhat pro-tected from hungry meal seekers as they flicker over the woodland floor.

Falcate Orangetip (female) on Yellow False Garlic

Falcate Orangetip caterpillar on toothwort

Falcate Orangetip caterpillar displaying false face

Thornlike Falcate
Orangetip chrysalid

Falcate Orangetip (female) on Yellow False Garlic

West Virginia White *Pieris virginiensis*

West Virginia Whites are at home in the Appalachian Mountain range. Its cool cove forests and rich deciduous woodlands are favorite haunts and breeding grounds. Fortunately for Alabamians, the northeast corner of our state includes just such habitats, allowing these delicate pierids to maintain residency.

West Virginia Whites are spring fliers, producing only one generation each year. Slowly fluttering over carpets of woodland wildflowers, they perpetually hunt for *white*, and white butterflies, white flowers—even white tennis shoes—capture their attention. Males search for white-winged females, but

West Virginia White (male) on Yellow False Garlic

females search for the white flowers of toothworts and cresses, their major host plants. Native members of the Mustard family, toothworts grow in concert with other spring-blooming wildflowers like trillium, hepatica, and bluebells. Females often stop to nectar at their hosts' small cross-shaped blossoms before depositing spindle-shaped eggs underneath chosen leaves. Caterpillars are downy and green, marked only with a faint lateral line. They complete development on a tight timetable because their meal-ticket toothworts are spring ephemerals, dying back to the ground soon after the season passes. Summer, fall, and winter are spent as chrysalides, attached by a girdle-like thread to more permanent structures.

West Virginia White populations have shown an alarming decline in the

West Virginia White (female) on Woodland Stonecrop

West Virginia White caterpillar on a toothwort

northeastern United States. One factor has been the invasion of Garlic-Mustard, a European species that escaped from cultivation in the 1860s and now carpets forest floors that previously supported toothwort colonies. Adding insult to injury, it contains mustard oils that entice female whites to oviposit on it, but caterpillars have not adapted to its particular chemical array and subsequently die when they eat it. At present, Alabama's rich northeastern forests have not succumbed, but the Alabama Exotic Pest Council places Garlic-Mustard on its Watch A List: "invasive in nearby states; has potential to be highly invasive in Alabama."[6]

West Virginia White nectaring on Woodland Stonecrop

Cabbage White *Pieris rapae*

European Cabbage Whites arrived in Toronto around 1860, found North America to their liking and made themselves permanent Alabama residents by 1881. Today they are some of our most common butterflies. Fluttering from early spring through late fall, they flourish statewide wherever mustard plants grow.

The widespread Mustard family is characterized by pungent juices and four-petaled, cross-shaped flowers. Our native white butterflies typically choose native mustards as larval hosts, but Cabbage Whites have a more cultivated palate and prefer introduced, engineered species that include broccoli, cauliflower, turnips, and of course, cabbage. In order to satisfy human taste buds, most of these food crops have been specifically developed to

Cabbage White
on mint

Above: Basking male
Cabbage White

Left: Caterpillar eating
cabbage

Left: Cabbage White chrysalid on Chinese Mustard

Below: Cabbage White on an aster

contain low levels of glucosinolate compounds known as mustard oil, which tastes bitter to humans, but stimulates egg laying in many pierids. These substances remain in adequate amounts for Cabbage Whites to detect, and females deposit eggs on almost any part of the plant. Emergent caterpillars have an appetite for foliage and are particularly disfiguring to cabbage as they bore into its leafy heads. The amount of mustard oil that is sequestered within larval bodies is uncertain, but caterpillars clearly do not rely on chemicals as their sole defense. While their unpleasant mustard taste may deter vertebrate predation, tiny body hairs are tipped with insecticidal oils called mayolenes that discourage ants and other invertebrate attackers. Caterpillars are also cryptically colored night eaters, suggesting that it is not advantageous to advertise a poisonous presence to predators. Chrysalides are colored for hiding: green if placed on a leaf, brown if attached to bark or other rough surfaces.

After a lifetime of relative invisibility, white-winged adults are not camouflaged in the least. Although their own chemical protection is thought to be minimal, they may benefit from looking like more unpalatable white butterflies that predators have learned to avoid.

Extremely common in agricultural areas, Cabbage Whites produce many overlapping broods and seem to be a constant presence. They also quickly colonize new areas, so no new garden is out of bounds. If all else fails, they are willing and able to make use of prolific, weedy mustards in vacant lots and newly disturbed areas. Established in Europe, Asia, Africa, and Australia, this well-adapted, highly adaptable immigrant is clearly here to stay.

Checkered White *Pontia protodice*

Checkered Whites are cloaked in mystery. Their life cycle is straightforward and seasonally ongoing. Their host plants are common weeds that quickly pop up and flourish after disturbances. They are sun-loving, nectar-drinking habitat generalists, yet their populations have declined dramatically in the last fifty years, and dedicated searches often end in disappointment. The question is, "Why?"

Many theories for Checkered Whites' presumed scarcity have been debated, with accusing fingers often pointed at Cabbage Whites—nonnative European immigrants whose populations swept through North America in

Above: Checkered White (female) ovipositing on Poorman's Pepperwort

Left: Checkered White (male) on an ironweed

the nineteenth century. Viewed as competitors for the same host plants, they are frequently vilified as plant-hogging, out-competing bullies. But Cabbage Whites typically choose cultivated, agricultural mustard species as their hosts, while Checkered Whites prefer wild and weedy mustards like Poorman's Pepperwort. Cabbage Whites are primarily leaf eaters, and Checkered Whites prefer a diet of buds, flowers, and seeds. The verdict is still out, but Cabbage Whites appear to be off the hook.

At least part of the answer to the Checkered White scarcity question may lie in their lifestyle, for these butterflies are opportunistic gypsies, constantly on the move, in search of the next patch of host plants. As a survival strategy, it works well, for their major mustard hosts are early succession annuals that quickly move in to colonize open, disturbed ground, but just as quickly disappear as more permanent vegetation takes hold.

Home-base populations do exist, and Checkered Whites should be sought in large fields and pastures. They may be easily misidentified as Cabbage Whites (perhaps another reason for their presumed scarcity). Females are easier to spot since their definitive charcoal checkering is more prominent.

Checkered Whites may be here today, gone tomorrow. Our first encounter with Checkered Whites was with a lone butterfly, captured and bound within a spider's web. Although the surrounding field was replete with pepperwort, no Checkered Whites had been seen before, and none have been seen since.

Checkered White (male)
on a frogfruit

Above: Checkered White caterpillar on Poorman's Pepperwort

Left: Checkered White chrysalid

Opposite: Checkered White (female) on an aster

Great Southern White *Ascia monuste*

In a state where there seems to be a pierid for every habitat, Great Southern Whites fill Alabama's coastal niche. Adapted to saltwater environments, these restless emigrants summer in south Alabama when warm temperatures allow them to move from their year-round Florida residences.

Great Southern Whites may be mistaken for more common Cabbage Whites. Both can be virtually solid-white butterflies, and their females display a similar black spot on their upper forewings. But Great Southerns sport vivid turquoise antennal clubs, and summer season females often assume a

Left: Great Southern White (male) on beggarticks

Below: Great Southern White (female) on Saltwort

dark or "nigra" form that sets them apart. Although they share a taste for many of the same Mustard family host plants preferred by Cabbage Whites, the mainstays of their diet are succulent crucifers like Coastal Sea-Rocket. Saltwort is also a frequent host. It is a member of the Batis family, but contains the all-important bitter mustard oils that stimulate females to oviposit. Pastel-yellow eggs are deposited singly or in small clusters on foliage and are impervious to salt water—an important adaptation in their often-maritime environments. Beautifully marked caterpillars gain a degree of distasteful toxicity from their diet, and adults join a group of other white butterflies that are similarly protected.

Caterpillar on
Saltwort

Great Southern White chrysalid attached to Poorman's Pepperwort

Like Checkered Whites, Great Southerns suffer from wanderlust. Individuals often disperse, but the species is known for massive emigrations where thousands leave to colonize new territory. Coastal movement is common, and some years they travel inland, utilizing many weedy mustard plants for reproduction. In the fall, there may be a backward trek as day lengths decrease. Freezing temperatures leave settlements only in more tropical climates, where Great Southern White pioneers wait for warm weather and crowded conditions to reinstate their northern expansion.

Above: Great Southern White female nectaring on beggarticks

Left: Great Southern White male on beggarticks

Puddling azures sip nutrients from damp sand.

Gossamer-Wings
The Lycaenidae

The Gossamer-Wings or lycaenids seem tiny and fragile, but their demeanors belie their delicate appearances. They are often aggressive and pugnacious, particularly when defending territories and searching for mates. Like many other butterflies, lycaenid wings are covered with two types of scales. Plain scale pigments form brown or gray hues, while iridescent colors are created by light refraction within structurally specialized scales. Female anatomy includes six normally sized legs: in males, the front pair is drastically reduced in size.

Lycaenid eggs are flattened discs, highly textured with pits and ridges. Caterpillars appear slug-like because of their tapered shape, but unlike slugs, they are covered with short hairs and their heads are often retracted within their bodies. Most prefer to eat flowering structures, including immature seeds or fruits. The larvae of many species engage in myrmecophily: literally, "ant-loving." Equipped with special glands (called Newcomer's organs) that produce sugary fluids, caterpillars receive protection from ants that are attracted to these sweet secretions. In addition, larval bodies also contain eversible, abdominal organs that may aid in communicating with their ant defenders.

Chrysalides are short, stout structures that are typically hidden in leaf litter or bark. Many reportedly produce squeaking sounds when disturbed, possibly creating a distress call to attendant ants. Some lycaenids hibernate in the pupal stage, but many overwinter as eggs, which are placed near future buds so that emergent caterpillars are strategically placed for prime eating opportunities. A few species spend the winter as larvae.

The Gossamer-Wings consist of four basic subgroups: the Harvesters, the Coppers, the Hairstreaks, and the Blues. North America's only Harvester species occurs sporadically throughout the East. Coppers and Blues are better represented in temperate northern regions, while Hairstreak populations are southern based.

Worldwide, the Harvesters live mainly in Africa and Asia. Only one species has found its way to North America. Harvester caterpillars are carnivorous and feed on woolly aphids. Butterflies also rely on aphid secretions (honey dew) as a primary energy source.

Although the Coppers are primarily northern butterflies, one (and occasionally two) species resides in Alabama. Known for the coppery iridescence on male dorsal wings, they frequently bask open-winged, which also reveals their females' plainer colors. Coppers typically live in local colonies near patches of their host plants, members of the Buckwheat family. As a rule, they are nonmigratory, so it is surprising that small colonies of Bronze Coppers occasionally turn up in north Alabama.

Most of the Hairstreaks have hindwing tails, and they use them to great advantage. Combined with nearby eyespots, antennae-like tails create a false head. The illusion is heightened by gentle hindwing rubbing motions and sometimes tricks predators into snapping at the butterfly's more expendable end, allowing those that keep their heads to fly away. Rapid, jerky flight styles also help hairstreaks escape from predators. Many hairstreaks use trees as host plants and often overwinter as strategically placed eggs. Some species are multibrooded, but many are univoltine: elfins fly only in the spring, while most satyriums emerge in early summer.

The Blues typically bask with open wings and display their namesake hue on upper surface (ventral) wings: they are often brown below. Sexually dimorphic, females are usually larger and duller, possessing little of their namesake color. The Blues are avid nectarers, but they also frequent puddle clubs. Legumes typically serve as caterpillar hosts. Most Blues overwinter as pupae, although a few reportedly spend the winter in larval form.

Opposite: Gray Hairstreak on Brazilian Vervain

Harvester *Feniseca tarquinius*

Harvesters are full of surprises. In a world where plant-animal relationships are all-important, rather than plants, Harvesters are directly dependent on other animals. Their carnivorous caterpillars (the only such beasts in the United States), have a sole diet of woolly aphids. Even adult butterflies shun flower nectar and primarily imbibe honeydew secreted by aphid survivors. Many references suggest that Harvesters should be sought near alders, but we suggest that they should be sought near colonies of woolly aphids.

Some woolly aphids resemble minuscule sheep—nothing more than cottony balls of fluff. Others, dubbed Boogie-Woogie aphids, seem to have stepped out of the pages of a Dr. Seuss book, waving pom-pom adorned posteriors in the air when disturbed. All are gregarious feeders, huddling

Harvester perching on
a cypress knee

together in flocklike groups. En masse, they look like cotton blankets and wrap around twigs and branches of host plants, which include well-known alders, as well as American Beech, American Witch-Hazel, and even Swamp Dogwood.

A female Harvester barely disturbs the aphid flock as she gently inserts her abdomen within it and deposits a minuscule white egg. Each explodes into a ravenous, meat-eating caterpillar. Larvae are sickly gray in color, but like the proverbial wolf in sheep's clothing, they quickly adorn themselves with fleecy castoffs from nearby aphids, and totally disappear in the crowd. In surprise attacks, they pick off aphids and devour them, with the remaining flock none the wiser. The reign of terror is brief, because their protein-rich diets enable Harvester caterpillars to complete development in only six days.

Chrysalides of the former aphid annihilators are also surprising. When in-

"Boogie-Woogie" aphids

specting the small, brown pupal structures, curious observers find that a tiny monkey's face or tribal mask seems to glare back from a sheltered twig or limb. Perhaps would-be predators think twice before engaging the mysterious creature attached to such a disturbing countenance.

Butterflies that emerge from the monkey-faced chrysalides pack surprises of their own. Short, squat, and stubby, they are amazingly fast and erratic

Left: Harvester caterpillar concealed in webbed nest constructed with cast-off woolly aphids' skins

Below: Harvester caterpillar eating woolly aphids

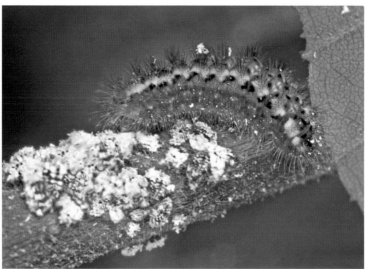

fliers. When disturbed or excited, they zing around like ricocheting bullets. It is a toss-up as to whether the term "whirling dervish" best describes the butterfly or the hapless lepidopterist who attempts to focus on it.

Predicting the presence of Harvesters is difficult since they are camp followers to their woolly aphid hosts. Usually encountered in ones or twos, spotting them on any field trip is always a lucky surprise.

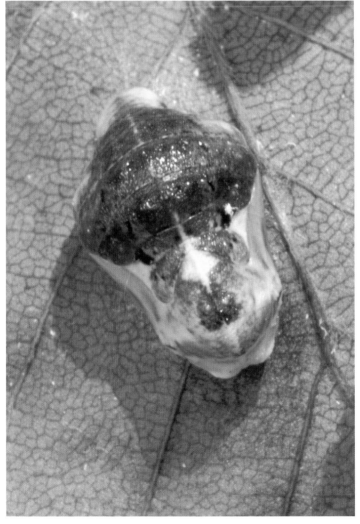

Harvester
chrysalid

American Copper *Lycaena phlaeas*

The American Copper's national origin is in question. Is it a native American butterfly or did it become American the same way many of this country's citizens did—by way of European immigration? Advocates of the "naturalized citizen" theory point out that our eastern population looks very different from its western American cousins but bears a strong resemblance to those in Europe. Opponents don't find the resemblance so striking. However, the real issue is not American Copper's appearance but its caterpillars' food preferences, for their primary host plant is Sheep Sorrel, a nonnative, European immigrant.

The plant in question is considered a weed by many and a scrawny one at that. Often standing only three or four inches high, Sheep Sorrel grows in disturbed areas that include fields, vacant lots, railways, and roadsides, and makes itself at home throughout the continental United States. It did not come to this country as an accidentally introduced weed but as an intentionally cultivated salad green. A bite of its tangy, lemon-flavored leaves explains why. This tart taste, a trademark of the Buckwheat family, comes from an abundance of oxalic acid. Sheep Sorrel is also high in antioxidants and has been described as antiseptic, antibacterial, antiviral, and antiparasitic.

Some of these "anti-agents" are the phytochemicals that induce female American Coppers to place their minute, disc-shaped eggs on the undersides of Sheep Sorrel and other buckwheat leaves. Tiny caterpillars first chew minuscule holes, but as they grow, their nibbles form distinct rectangular channels. To avoid predators that would recognize this telltale pattern, caterpillars "eat and run," moving down the plant's base to distance themselves from clever hunters. Camouflage is another defense mechanism. Some caterpillars are uniformly leaf-green, matching the color of a healthy, happy sorrel plant. However, during dry spells, chlorophyll content becomes significantly depleted, and sorrel leaves and stems become heavily suffused with red. Coppers have this color variant covered, for within their caterpillar populations,

Opposite: American Copper sipping from White Crownbeard

some are solid green, others are rose-tinged, and still others are completely red. When pupation time arrives, final instars curl a leaf, web it with silk, and crawl inside. Their final molt and the resulting chrysalides are hidden with the leafy structure.

Male American Coppers are notoriously aggressive in their pursuit of females. They fixedly pursue the subject of sex, settling down only briefly to nectar at various small flowers. Like eternal optimists, they dart from low plant perches to check out any moving object, be it falling leaf, fluttering monarch, or intrepid butterflier. The distinguished lepidopterist Alexander Klots reports that one little guy even buzzed an airplane.

Above: Rose-tinged American Copper caterpillar on Sheep Sorrel

Opposite: American Copper caterpillar camouflaged on Sheep Sorrel

Above: American Copper chrysalid

Opposite: American Copper on White Crownbeard

Bronze Copper *Lycaena hyllus*

Who would guess that Bronze Coppers would make the list of Alabama butterflies? They typically range from central North America northward into Canada. Yet verified sightings confirm that, regardless of what range maps indicate, they also occupy portions of northeast Alabama.

It's not a case of mistaken identity. Bronze Coppers bear a strong resemblance to American Coppers, but they are noticeably larger. In fact, they are the largest of the eastern coppers. Their common name is a nod to the coppery upper surfaces of the males, often washed with a violet sheen that adds the "bronzed" effect. Females are plainer above, but share the male's lovely tangerine and gray ventral coloration. Hindwings are edged with a broad orange band, which along with their larger overall size helps identifiers distinguish Bronze Coppers from others within the group.

The Bronze Copper is a "fugitive" species—one that disappears quickly as succession progresses past its earliest stages. Its habitats are ephemeral and almost completely dependent on some form of disturbance for creation and maintenance. While many butterflies are linked to transient habitats, Bronze Coppers require early succession *wetland* sites, a particularly difficult niche to find.

Within their wet and weedy habitats, Bronze Coppers look for tall Buckwheat family plants like Curly Dock and Swamp Dock, their favored host plants. Knotweeds also serve as larval feeding stations in some parts of the country, but the host of choice in Alabama is currently unknown. Females scatter their turban-shaped eggs on the undersides of leaves, along stems, and sometimes on seed heads. Caterpillars are primarily leaf eaters, but will also devour buds and flowers. They are cryptically colored to match their yellow-green hosts. Although highly camouflaged, a distinctive eating pattern provides clues to their presence. As caterpillars chew, they form narrow grooves in tender host leaves. On tougher, more mature leaves, larvae only scrape the surface, creating a transparent windowpane effect. Chrysalides may be attached to their host plants and are green or tan with dark speckles. Like their hosts, they are sometimes suffused with red. Bronze Coppers typically overwinter as eggs.

Bronze Copper on Common Milkweed

From top:

Bronze Copper (male) basking

Bronze Copper (female) on a daisy fleabane

Bronze Copper caterpillar on Curly Dock

Male butterflies are often encountered as they perch on foliage to wait for females, frequently staking their claim on a substantial blade of grass. In typical copper fashion, they sit with partially opened wings, allowing good looks at their upper surface sheen. Both sexes nectar on small flowers, including blossoms like milkweed that are clustered together in dense heads or inflorescences.

Throughout much of their eastern range, Bronze Copper populations are declining, presumably due to habitat loss. In Alabama, their toehold is tenuous. Our known Bronze Copper colony is dependent on the fortunes of on-again, off-again low-lying cotton fields. When the fields lie barren, dock plants pop up, and so do Bronze Coppers. In years that cotton replaces dock, the coppers seem to vanish—a frustrating scenario. However, without the cycle of disturbance and renewal, plant succession would progress to stages unfavorable to this wide-ranging but apparently very exacting species, and Bronze Coppers might disappear altogether.

Bronze Copper chrysalid

Great Purple Hairstreak *Atlides halesus*

Great Purples are giants among hairstreaks. Largest of the group within Alabama, they are not only big, but also beautiful. Their folded wings display harlequin colors of orange, red, blue, and bronze, and their tails are long and graceful. Because upperwings contain structural color scales that reflect light, flight is accentuated with flashes of electric blue. Males possess more brightly colored wings, but both sexes flaunt orange bodies, signaling would-be predators that their taste may not be pleasant.

If Great Purple Hairstreaks are indeed poisonous, American Mistletoe is the source of their toxicity. It contains a bevy of phytochemicals, including calcium oxalate crystals that can cause intense burning sensations even in small doses. Great Purples are the only butterflies that have adapted to its particular chemical array, and their caterpillars will eat nothing else. Partially parasitic on several hardwood trees (including oaks), "Christmas" mistletoe's familiar clumps are exposed only during fall and winter when tree branches are otherwise bare. Great Purples actively seek these hitchhiking semi-parasites during spring, summer, and fall, and even nectar on their inconspicuous, stem-hugging flowers.

Great Purple Hairstreaks spend much of their time in treetops, where females place single eggs within clusters of mistletoe. Slug-shaped larvae eat flowers and foliage, closely mimicking leaves with their thickly rounded shapes and mottled green coloring. Young larvae prefer young, tender leaves and are only capable of scraping outer layers of those that are thicker and more mature. Later instars may bore into foliage before devouring it completely. Fully grown caterpillars descend trees to form coffee-beanish pupae under scaly bark or on leaf litter near the trunk. Three generations occur, and chrysalides overwinter.

Observers often count themselves fortunate to find even one Great Purple Hairstreak, but late summer and early fall offer opportunities to see larger

Opposite: Great Purple Hairstreak nectaring on White Crownbeard

Great Purple Hairstreak caterpillar camouflaged on American Mistletoe

numbers of these gorgeous butterflies. Fall-blooming wildflowers like Climbing Hempvine, White Crownbeard, and goldenrods are irresistible to Great
Purples and draw them down from tree canopies. Deliberate and docile, they
frequently remain on flower heads for long periods, exploring inflorescences
from every angle and methodically sipping from each tiny nectary.

Great Purple Hairstreak chrysalid hidden in leaf litter

Coral Hairstreak *Satyrium titus*

Butterfly Milkweed is a magnet for Coral Hairstreaks. In fact, one of the best ways to search for the hairstreaks is to first locate patches of orange milkweed flowers along deciduous woodland edges. Its bloom time signals that the hunt should begin, for the Coral Hairstreaks' once-a-year flight coincides with the Butterfly Milkweeds' early summer flowers.

As fond as Coral Hairstreaks are of Butterfly Milkweed, it serves only as a nectar source. Host plant distinction goes to Black Cherry and other native cherries and plums, all members of the Rose family. Female Corals often deposit their flattened white eggs at the base of young trees, in cracks and crevices or underneath peeling bark. Eggs remain hidden until the following spring when tiny larvae emerge and begin their arduous journey up the tree in search of tender flower buds and emergent leaves. It is a trip they will make often, for they are reportedly night eaters and conceal themselves back at the tree's foot during daylight hours. Ant comrades, which provide guard services in return for caterpillars' sweet secretions, may accompany them. As larval development continues, camouflage also aids in protection from predators. Basically green, caterpillar heads and tails are saturated with patches of the same rosy hues that suffuse cherry leaves and stems. Late in spring, chrysalid placement requires a final excursion down the tree so that last-instar caterpillars can locate just the right spot in nearby leaf litter for their pupal transformations.

Coral Hairstreaks are often found in the company of other satyrium hairstreaks, but Corals are less tied to the woods than their cousins and more likely to venture into open, sunny areas. While most satyrium hairstreaks are double-tailed, basically brown, and notoriously difficult to identify, Coral Hairstreak identification is easy. Totally tailless, they also flaunt a row of bright-orange spots on their hindwings, reminiscent of—you guessed it—Butterfly Milkweed.

Left: Coral Hairstreak on Butterfly Milkweed

Below: Caterpillar on Black Cherry

Edwards' Hairstreak *Satyrium edwardsii*

At first glance, Edwards' Hairstreaks seem like any other satyrium hairstreak. They display the same gray-brown wing color, and it is punctuated with the same array of spots and dots that must be sorted out in order to make a positive identification. They are univoltine and fly in the same early summer satyrium time slot. They visit the same flower species for nectar (Butterfly Milkweed is a favorite), and caterpillars share the basic slug-shaped appearance of all the others in the group. But, these seemingly ordinary caterpillars engage in a bizarre lifestyle that places Edwards' Hairstreak in a category all its own.

The story begins predictably. Edwards' caterpillars hatch from eggs deposited the previous year on twigs of young scrub oaks. The tiny larvae hide under foliage during daylight hours and at night emerge to eat catkins and young leaves. As they grow, they develop organs that secrete sugary substances that are extremely attractive to ants. Recognizing a good thing when they taste it, ants defend caterpillars against predators and parasites. So far, the scenario is common to many ant-tended hairstreaks and blues. But at this point, the story takes a Ripley's Believe It or Not twist. Upon reaching third instar, caterpillars leave their scrub-oak leaves as daylight approaches and, along with attendant ants, journey down the trunk. Rather than resting at the bottom, they are herded into byres (literally, "cow stalls"), loosely mounded formations constructed by ants at the sapling's base. Aboveground, the byres appear to be heaps of woodland detritus, but underground they form a veritable labyrinth of chambers. In addition to inactive caterpillars, ants may also herd treehopper nymphs (another source of sugary secretions) into their byres. As evening falls, closely guarded caterpillars climb back up the tree to resume their nocturnal feeding routine. Night after night, they make their journey upward, and day after day, they return to their chambers, never far from solicitous ants. When larval development is complete, caterpillars make a final trip down the trunk, crawl into the byre and settle in for pupation. Lined up like mummies in an underground tomb, several chrysalides may

Left: Caterpillar ascending scrub oak at dusk (photo by Jeffrey Glassberg)

Right: Chrysalid with a wood ant

occupy the same cavity, sometimes a foot or more from the tree. Approximately ten days later, when metamorphosis is complete, butterflies emerge in the dark hole. Fresh, wet-winged Edwards' Hairstreaks must crawl through subterranean tunnels before surfacing to fresh air and sunlight.

Much remains to be learned about the exact relationships between the hairstreaks, oaks, ants, and nymphs. It is possible that each element represents an Edwards' Hairstreak habitat necessity. These unique butterflies sometimes find all the essentials in parts of eastern Alabama, where their populations are uncommon and local.

Edwards' Hairstreak on Butterfly Milkweed

Banded Hairstreak *Satyrium calanus*

Bandeds are quintessential satyrium hairstreaks in both appearance and life-style. As a group, satyriums are identification nightmares: all display gray-brown wings decorated only with various arrays of dots and dashes. Positive identification depends on field-mark nuances. Banded Hairstreaks' blue hind-wing dots are not capped with red, but thankfully, their white dashes merge to form very visible namesake bands. Like their fellow satyriums, Bandeds are univoltine. Winter is spent in egg form, caterpillars hatch in early spring, and butterflies emerge by early summer.

Most male satyrium hairstreaks are pugnacious territory defenders, but Bandeds take this behavior to a new level: their aerial dogfights are legend-ary. The males tirelessly dart at and swirl with other encroaching males, and encounters routinely last for several minutes. Combatants momentarily sep-arate only to go at each other again. Undaunted, they eventually retreat to the same, eye-level perch and resume sentry duty.

Banded males are commonly encountered along woodland trails and openings where they strategically place themselves to watch for females and to defend their territory. Female Bandeds make themselves scarce (perhaps to avoid the onslaught of male attentions), and are most often discovered at good nectaring sites. Both sexes tank up at satyrium flower favorites like Butterfly Milkweed, Yellow Sweet-Clover, and Common New Jersey-Tea, as well as canopy-blooming Sourwood. Early mornings and late afternoons are favorite feeding times.

Like most egg-overwintering butterflies (including other satyrium hair-streaks), Bandeds select deciduous trees as their larval hosts rather than ephemeral, herbaceous plants. Oaks and hickories are well-known choices, but within this broad group, accurate observations are needed to determine which species they prefer in Alabama. Whatever constitutes the perfect oak or hickory tree, when a female Banded finds it, she painstakingly places her eggs on twigs and branches, near locations that will be near next year's cat-kins (oak/hickory flowering structures). Emergent caterpillars are typical hairstreak bud/flower/young leaf eaters, but they display a bewildering col-

Left: Banded Hairstreak on Butterfly Milkweed

Below: Banded Hairstreak caterpillars displaying different color forms

lection of color forms, running the gamut from creamy catkin white and oak-leaf green all the way to hickory-twig brown. Bark-brown pupal color suggests that caterpillars transform into chrysalides among leaf litter or within tree crevices.

Oak-Hickory forests are common and widespread throughout much of Alabama. Suitable habitat is not lacking, and Bandeds are our most numerous satyrium hairstreaks.

King's Hairstreak *Satyrium kingi*

King's Hairstreaks are host plant and habitat specialists. While they look like other satyrium hairstreaks and share their basic life cycle, King's Hairstreaks deviate from their cousins' use of widespread, common-as-dirt deciduous host trees. Their caterpillars eat only Horse-Sugar, a semi-evergreen, understory inhabitant of streamsides, wooded swamps, and riverbanks.

Horse-Sugar does not seem to fit the bill for a hairstreak host. Its yellow pom-pom flowers are composed primarily of stamens that could potentially offer nourishment to bud-eating hairstreak larvae, but blossoms occur in very early spring and are long gone before caterpillars hatch. King's Hairstreak caterpillars reportedly refuse flowers anyway, preferring an exclusive diet of leaves. Horse-Sugar's almost-evergreen foliage is extremely tough and leathery, but timing is everything. After retaining its leaves for months, it drops them in late winter/very early spring. New foliage follows flowers and is soft and chewable: perfect food for growing caterpillars. Larvae are colored for camouflage and often sit invisibly underneath leaves, munching away in the weeks before vegetation becomes fully mature and hardened.

Because of its habitat restrictions, King's Hairstreaks often find that nectar sources are limited. Few plants bloom in early summer; especially in the shady woodlands these hairstreaks call home. Sourwood, late-blooming Virginia Sweetspire, and Sparkleberry are potential nectar sources.

Diligent searchers may spot triangular King's Hairstreak silhouettes as the small butterflies perch in patches of sunlight on their host plants' perpetually droopy leaves. Long considered rare and reclusive, they may not be so uncommon in their preferred habitats. Perhaps King's Hairstreaks are like Horse-Sugar, which, according to the beloved Alabama botanist Blanche E. Dean, "grows over most of Alabama but does not seem to be well known."[7]

Clockwise from top:

King's Hairstreak on
Virginia Sweetspire

Chrysalid on
Horse-Sugar

Caterpillar on
partially eaten
Horse-Sugar leaf

Striped Hairstreak *Satyrium liparops*

At first glance, Striped Hairstreaks are typical satyriums. Like the others, they are basically brown butterflies: unmarked or plainly marked above; decorated with a blue dot, a few red spots, and white dashes below. And like their cousins, they are univoltine, flying only a few weeks in early summer and overwintering as eggs. But in spite of their similarities, Striped Hairstreaks are also markedly different. They prefer more wooded habitats and seldom engage in the pugnacious dogfights so typical of their genus. Rarely seen in numbers, they seem quiet and retiring by comparison.

Throughout their range, many members of the Heath and Rose families are reported as Striped Hairstreaks' hosts, including Black Cherry and hawthorns. In central Alabama, we have found their caterpillars eating native blueberries and huckleberries, both members of the Heath family. Eggs are tucked into bud and leaf nodes during early summer, but do not hatch until early spring the following year. Since first instars may emerge before flower buds significantly swell, hungry caterpillars sometimes bore into tightly pointed leaf buds to gain initial nourishment. Eventually they consume buds, flowers, and developing fruits. Yellow-green larvae easily fade into blueberry foliage, and when devouring the white, bell-shaped blossoms, they appear to be green sepals attached at the flowers' base.

A good stand of Sparkleberry, a native blueberry, provides almost everything a Striped Hairstreak needs. Males perch at eye level on branches to search for females, and females search deep within branches for nodes and crevices in which to place overwintering eggs. Sparkleberry's small flower clusters are Striped Hairstreak favorites, but other nectar sources include milkweeds, sourwoods, and privets.

When looking at a group of satyrium hairstreaks, Striped Hairstreaks are among the easiest to identify. They are marked with uniformly aligned, white-outlined bars. In a confusing array of dotted and dashed satyrium hairstreak wings, these telltale stripes are easily seen, much-appreciated field marks.

Opposite: Striped Hairstreak perched on a blueberry

Above: Late instar Sriped Hairstreak caterpillar eating a blueberry flower

Left: Sriped Hair-streak chrysalid on a blueberry leaf

Opposite: Early instar Sriped Hairstreak caterpillar resting on a blueberry stem after exiting upper leaf bud

Oak Hairstreak *Satyrium favonius*

Oak Hairstreaks are an enigma. Their range is statewide, their host plants are common, yet sightings are spotty, and colonies seem transient. Just because they are found one year, does not mean they will be in the same spot the next—a point painfully hammered home when a small colony discovered in my Birmingham yard in 2001 disappeared the following year. As of this writing, it is still missing in action.

Oak Hairstreaks have also led taxonomists on a merry chase. Initially described in 1797, species definition remains a source of heated disagreement and contention. What exactly *is* an Oak Hairstreak? Currently, prevailing thought is that two distinct subspecies occur, different in appearance, range

"Northern" Oak Hairstreak on Sparkleberry

and, to some extent, lifestyle. "Southern" Oak Hairstreaks populate Florida and coastal Georgia and display an extensive flame of red on their hindwings. "Northern" Oak Hairstreaks, which occupy most of Alabama, are plainer, and the red marking is reduced to little more than an ember. As if not complicated enough, a geographic blend zone occurs where individuals display intermediate markings. Deep south Alabama falls within this zone, and butterflies representing all three forms may be found there.

Oak Hairstreaks are single-brooded, flying in late spring, usually a couple of weeks before other satyrium hairstreaks. Named for their larval hosts, several oak species nourish caterpillars, including giant live oaks and white oaks. Adult butterflies spend much of their day in host treetops (perhaps one reason they are seldom encountered), so observing their aerial antics

"Southern" Oak Hairstreak on Sparkleberry

requires strong binoculars as well as strong neck muscles. Females deposit rusty-brown, Frisbee-shaped eggs on twigs, often in crooks or scars, where they remain unhatched throughout the weather extremes of three seasons. Egg diapause is broken ten months later, and tiny caterpillars emerge in early spring when oak catkins and new leaves begin to swell. Larvae initially bore into developing oak flowers to dine on protein-rich, embryonic pollen. As the season progresses, young leaves provide their menu's final course. When caterpillar development is complete, slug-shaped larvae form brown, pellet-shaped chrysalides at the tree's base or in nearby leaf litter. New Oak Hair-streaks emerge about two weeks later, completing a life cycle that required almost a year to reach fruition.

Live Oak catkins with hole eaten by the early instar Oak Hairstreak caterpillar

Oak Hairstreak caterpillar eating Live Oak catkins

Oak Hairstreak chrysalid on leaf litter

Juniper Hairstreak *Callophrys gryneus*

Red-cedars are home base for Juniper Hairstreaks. One of only three but-terfly species in the Southeast that produces conifer-eating caterpillars, it is closely tied to landscapes that support its sole larval host. Because of this intimate association with red-cedar, Juniper Hairstreaks are at home in Ala-bama's most common habitats (roadsides, old fields, and pasture edges) as well as its most rare (blackland prairies, granite outcrops, and cedar glades).

Juniper Hairstreaks and red-cedars share an olive-green, rusty-red color palette. When nectaring on bright-yellow flowers, butterflies appear star-tlingly green, but perched on cedar twigs, they blend invisibly with its foliage. They are so difficult to detect that the time-honored method for locating Ju-niper Hairstreaks involves vigorously shaking or tapping cedar trees, causing butterflies to swirl up before re-alighting.

Viewed out of cedar context, Juniper Hairstreak caterpillars appear ex-travagantly patterned and highly ornamented, but on a cedar twig, they defy

Juniper Hairstreak on Woolly Ragwort

detection. Broken green stripes blend with fingerlike cedar needles. Even scaly larval texture closely resembles tips and points of cedar foliage. Unlike clothes moths that are repelled by pungent cedar oil, Juniper Hairstreak larvae readily digest it, along with other natural pesticides found in red-cedars' stiff and prickly foliage. Three generations are produced in much of Alabama, so hairstreak-hosting red-cedars are seldom without tiny green munchers.

Chrysalid placement is also integrally tied to red-cedars' shape and growth habits. When allowed to retain their natural forms, cedar branches gently droop, almost brushing the ground. As slow-growing trees mature, years of discarded, decay-resistant foliage and berries called "duff" accumulate underneath. Amid this protective blanket, last instar caterpillars search for the perfect spot to pupate. Recent research in Florida reveals that the common practice of "limbing up" cedar trees renders them useless as Juniper Hairstreak hosts. Female butterflies choose only naturally formed, duff-rich trees for egg placement, illustrating once again the intricate and subtle interdependencies that exist in the natural world.

A highly camouflaged caterpillar on Eastern Red-Cedar

Hessel's Hairstreak *Callophrys hesseli*

Somewhere within Alabama's remaining stands of Atlantic White-Cedar, Hessel's Hairstreaks fly. Across the state line, in Florida's Blackwater State Forest, localized populations are well documented, but although many range maps indicate that these dark-green butterflies extend into Alabama, we reported the first sighting on March 31, 2010. The scarcity of Hessel's Hairstreaks comes as no surprise, for (to borrow a phrase) as Atlantic White-Cedar goes, so goes Hessel's Hairstreak, and Atlantic White-Cedar habitats have all but vanished within our state.

Only since 1950 have Hessel's Hairstreaks been recognized as separate entities from more common and wide-ranging Juniper Hairstreaks. Although the two olive-green species bear a marked resemblance, there are reliable field marks that separate them: one of the most reliable is Hessel's offset forewing dash (in Juniper, these dashes form a straight line). Their appearances may be similar, but host plant and habitat choices are decidedly different—and Hessel's drew the short straw.

The Juniper Hairstreak's common host, the Eastern Red-Cedar grows throughout Alabama. It is a common, early succession pioneer and sprouts everywhere from country fencerows to highway roadsides. Hessel's Hairstreak caterpillars feed exclusively on Atlantic White-Cedar, a wetland conifer that requires both fire and flooding for regeneration and is found only in Washington, Mobile, Baldwin, and Escambia counties. Much more common at the time of European settlement, Atlantic White-Cedar was (and is) considered valuable timber due to its lightweight, rot-resistant wood, and stands were logged extensively throughout the last two centuries. Loss of wetlands to development, altered water flow, fire suppression, and poor logging practices have all played a part in drastically depleting Alabama's Atlantic White-Cedar populations.

When they can find them, Hessel's Hairstreaks deposit flattened pale

Opposite: Hessel's Hairstreak perched on Atlantic White-Cedar

green eggs on the growing tips of Atlantic White-Cedar branches. Initially, tiny caterpillars appear to be a single flake of foliage, and as they grow, their coloration provides remarkable camouflage. As green as their cedar hosts, they are also ornamented with pale chevrons that give the illusion of overlapping cedar scales. A spring and summer brood occurs, and winter is spent as a bark-brown chrysalid.

Males devote their time to typical hairstreak pursuits: perching on twigs to await females, engaging in aerial dogfights with other males, re-alighting on the same perch to await females. Unfortunately for human observers, these activities often occur fifty feet in the air. Butterflies typically descend to the ground shortly after first light, and both males and females can be found along roadways near their chosen cedar trees. Hessel's Hairstreaks also derive energy from nectar. To date we have documented use of spring-blossoming Black Titi in Alabama.

"As Atlantic White-Cedar goes, so goes Hessel's Hairstreak." But help may be on the way. Thanks to an agreement with International Paper Company, the Nature Conservancy has acquired approximately 14,000 acres of the Perdido River corridor that it will ultimately turn over to the state. Added to the holdings of Alabama's Forever Wild Program, as much as twenty miles of river frontage will be in conservation and a large percentage will contain Atlantic White-Cedars. If habitat restoration efforts are successful, more thriving colonies of Hessel's Hairstreak may ultimately be discovered in Alabama.

A highly camouflaged Hessel's Hairstreak caterpillar on Atlantic White-Cedar

Brown Elfin *Callophrys augustinus*

Brown Elfins are Alabama's plainest elfins—no tails or frostings liven up their look. Still, when freshly emerged, they are sedately handsome butterflies with rich chestnut and mahogany wings that sometimes display a purplish sheen. Although records in Alabama are sparse, sightings in Mississippi and recent finds in Florida indicate that they could occur almost anywhere in the state that the habitat is right. Look for them in dry forests that support pines, oaks, and evergreen heaths such as blueberries and laurels. Like all elfins, they are univoltine and fly only in spring (generally March and April).

Brown Elfin host plants belong to the Heath family—herbs, shrubs, and trees that thrive in acidic soils. Many familiar plants are heaths, including blueberries, huckleberries, and azaleas. Brown Elfins often use various blue-berries (or vacciniums) as larval hosts, but in Florida and North Carolina, they also choose Mountain-Laurel, shrubs that may also support Brown Elfins in Alabama. Like other elfins, Brown Elfin caterpillars eat flowering structures whenever they are available, and their flattened, disc-shaped eggs are often deposited on buds. Yellow-green larvae bore into these immature flowers in order to reach developing pollen granules, which are extremely rich in pro-tein. As the bloom cycle ends, so does the caterpillars' eating phase. Light-brown chrysalides rest within ground litter and are the overwintering stage of the Brown Elfins' life cycle.

Brown Elfins nectar at small spring flowers that range from plums and redbuds to low-growing phloxes. Blueberry blossoms are also favorite adult energy sources. Brown Elfins are generally found along woodland edges, openings, and trails, where males perch on low twigs to await females, and frequently engage in aggressive aerial disputes with other males. They con-gregate on the ground during morning hours to sip from damp soil. Often found in the company of other elfins, observers should look carefully for small, tailless butterflies within a group of more highly ornamented compan-ions.

Brown Elfin perched on a phlox

Above: Brown Elfin caterpillar eating Mountain-Laurel

Opposite: Brown Elfin chrysalid in leaf litter

Frosted Elfin *Callophrys irus*

Frosted Elfins are rare throughout their range. Populations have plummeted during the past fifty years. According to NatureServe's conservation data,[8] at least seven states rank them as critically imperiled, including neighboring Florida. More states list Frosted Elfins as a "species of concern" than any other nonfederally listed species, and no state that counts them as resident considers them secure. Although their current status in Alabama is classified as "under review," we know of only one record of Frosted Elfin within the state. That specimen was collected in Tuscaloosa County during the 1950s and is currently housed at the Alabama Museum of Natural History.

Frosted Elfins are small, brown butterflies with short tails and extensive clouding or "frosting" on their hindwings. Similar in appearance to Henry's Elfin, a small hindwing spot (located near the outer margin) is diagnostic. Habitat distinctions are extremely important: Henry's Elfins are common woodland fliers, but Frosted Elfins are definitely not.

Frosted Elfins require highly specialized habitat. Their populations depend on early succession plant communities that contain lupine or wild indigo species—unique sites that were historically maintained by fire. As succession progressed and sun-loving host plants were shaded and replaced by a layer of shrubs, Frosted Elfins moved to the next burned patch. Unfortunately, today these habitats are highly fragmented and almost nonexistent. Most Frosted Elfin habitat is now confined to remnant natural sites or man-made landscapes like powerline cuts, railroad edges, or airport runways—all of which typically depend on haphazard management.

Like all elfins, Frosteds produce only one brood each year. Butterflies are on the wing for approximately a six-week period in spring. Caterpillars consume either lupines or wild indigos (baptisias). Both are nitrogen-fixing legumes, and both contain lupanine, a toxic alkaloid. Lupine-eating elfins tuck their eggs into unopened bud clusters. Tiny caterpillars first chew pinprick holes into developing buds, crawl inside, and eventually hollow out the interior. Older larvae bore bigger holes and ultimately decimate entire buds, flowers, or seedpods. Wild indigo feeders are more likely to select a diet of

Frosted Elfin perched on stem

young leaves. Chrysalides of both types overwinter at the host plant's base, although pupae formed by lupine feeders may be partially submerged in the ground, protecting them from seasonal fires.

In spite of the fact that Frosted Elfins are "rare, imperiled or extirpated in all states," all is not lost. According to NatureServe, they are "not imminently imperiled everywhere and there are reasonably secure populations in a few states."[9] Some habitats can even be recovered. Although the Frosted Elfins' status in Alabama is currently unknown, diligent searches of appropriate habitat may find that they still exist outside museum walls.

Frosted Elfin caterpillar resting on Southern Sundial Lupine after molting

Frosted Elfin caterpillar near a partially eaten Oak Ridge Lupine flower

Henry's Elfin on Eastern Redbud

Henry's Elfin *Callophrys henrici*

"Look for Henry's Elfins when redbuds bloom." The respected Georgia lepidopterist Irving Finkelstein once shared this wisdom with us, and over the years, it has proven true. Blue phloxes and trilliums are also tip-offs, for Henry's Elfins are solely spring fliers, heralds of the season along with Spring Azures and first-generation tiger swallowtails.

Spring is the season for Henry's Elfins, and the woods are their habitat. Sometimes known as "Woodland Elfin," the characteristics of Henry's Elfins' forested environments vary depending on which host plant they choose. As a species, Henry's Elfin is comprised of several geographically separated subspecies, and each selects a specific plant family for feeding its caterpillars. Much remains to be learned about these host preferences, but at least two subspecies occur in Alabama.

Coastal Plain Henry's Elfin caterpillars are holly eaters. Inhabiting floodplains and wetlands, American Holly is a frequent choice, and eggs are deposited on swelling flower buds or very new leaves. Hungry caterpillars bore into embryonic blossoms, robbing the Christmas landscape of a few red berries but allowing access to nutritious pollen grains. When pupation time arrives in late spring, rather than heading exclusively for protective soil and leaf litter, caterpillars sometimes choose higher ground, attaching themselves to

Caterpillar
on American
Holly

tree trunks in this potentially flooded environment. The mottled brown chrysalides must survive until spring's return the following year.

In other regions of Alabama, Henry's Elfins choose drier, upland woods where plant communities typically include white oaks, hickories, and cedars. Definitive host-plant choice is unknown, but native blueberries and Eastern Redbuds are selected in nearby states.

Wherever they live, Henry's Elfins spend the majority of their time in trees: perching, ovipositing, and nectaring. They descend in morning hours to take

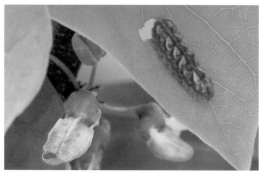

Above: Henry's Elfin chrysalid in leaf litter

Left: Henry's Elfin caterpillar eating Eastern Redbud

moisture and minerals from the ground. Often encountered along woodland paths, males aggressively defend small territories. Swirling dogfights with other elfins or an occasional skipper may last several minutes, with the victor returning to his previous perch. Henry's Elfins acquire nectar from an array of blossoms, which they often find on flowering trees. In wetland areas, Horse-Sugar is a magnet, while flowering plums are chosen in drier habitats. And it is fitting that the Eastern Redbud, a harbinger of Henry's Elfin flight, is also a favorite nectar source.

Henry's Elfin (male) perching on a pine

Eastern Pine Elfin *Callophrys niphon*

Eastern Pine Elfins don't quite fit the elfin mold. Alabama's other three elfin species are nubby-tailed, muddy-brown butterflies, similar enough in appearance to present identification problems. Eastern Pine Elfin wings are totally tailless and highly patterned with busy chevrons. Given a good look, they are unmistakable. Like all elfins, Eastern Pines are single-brooded spring fliers, but they tend to emerge later in the season and fly considerably longer than their relatives. In Alabama, they have been observed well into May, a late date for elfins.

Pine elfins are also unique in their host plant choice. They are conifer eaters: the only butterfly species that chooses pines as its larval food. Female Eastern Pine Elfins lay eggs on fresh young needles of "hard" pines such as

Eastern Pine Elfin on a flowering plum

Loblolly and Virginia pines. Early instar caterpillars eat needle sheaths, precisely duplicating their rusty-red color. Final instars devour entire needles. Tightly grasping the shafts with their legs, they start at the top and methodically munch down to the base. Bold stripes provide camouflage, and caterpillars blend with linearly patterned pine foliage.

Despite an apparent abundance of suitable habitat, pine elfins are rarely encountered in numbers. Although they generally stick close to their piney woods, they venture out to nectar and to sip minerals from puddles along trails and rural roadways. Eastern Pine Elfins seldom live in the middle of "pine plantation" monocultures. They choose more biologically diverse edge habitats that support an array of spring-flowering nectar sources in addition to their namesake pines.

Early instar
caterpillar highly
camouflaged
on tallest pine
needle sheath

Final instar Eastern Pine Elfin caterpillar eating pine needles

Eastern Pine Elfin chrysalid in leaf litter

Red-Banded Hairstreak *Calycopsis cecrops*

Red-Banded Hairstreaks often materialize out of nowhere, suddenly appearing on the ground, perched on leaves, or nectaring on flower heads. Because male interior wings are coated with iridescent scales, a small flash of metallic blue frequently announces their seemingly teleported entrances and exits. Both male and female butterflies display a distinctive red band, their most apparent field mark. This zigzagged line comes in any shade of red (up to and including orange), and may be broadly stroked or pencil thin. It separates Red-Bandeds from all other hairstreaks in Alabama.

Red-Banded Hairstreaks are habitat generalists and widely occur across the state. They are common in both wet and dry sites and occupy wooded as well as open areas. While sunny areas are preferred, we have encountered them on many occasions in deeply shaded forests. They are avid nectarers,

Red-Banded Hairstreak on Common White Snakeroot

Rubbing their wings together reveals a male Red-Banded Hairstreak's blue upper surface or a female's brown upper surface

and often drink from sumac blossoms, as well as milkweeds, mountain-mints, goldenrods, and crownbeards.

Red-Bandeds add an interesting plot twist to the familiar caterpillar-host-plant story. Rather than eating fresh young leaves, their caterpillars typically eat decaying ones. Females often deposit their disc-shaped eggs on fallen leaves of a variety of host plants, with sumacs, wax-myrtles, and oaks heading the list. Subsequently, caterpillars eat deteriorating foliage within the ground litter. Colored accordingly, they are dark, dirt-brown and disappear into plant detritus. Fuzzy brown chrysalides are also well concealed in ground debris.

Red-Banded Hairstreaks produce several distinct broods in Alabama. Occasionally, large outbreaks occur when they seem to be everywhere. They are common inhabitants of fall flowering fields. Months later, when dozens nectar amid wild plum blossoms, these tiny unexpected hairstreaks provide a welcomed sign of spring.

Red-Banded Hairstreak caterpillar in sumac detritus

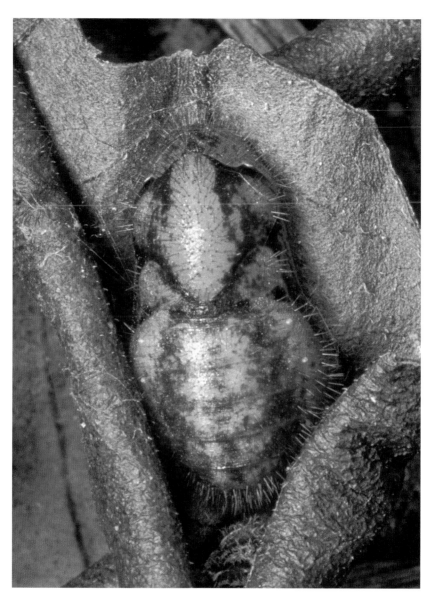

Red-Banded Hairstreak chrysalid

Gray Hairstreak *Strymon melinus*

Beside the word "widespread" in the dictionary, look for Gray Hairstreak's picture. (Other frequently used adjectives include "common" and "ubiquitous.") North Carolina Natural Heritage Program's Harry LeGrand laments, "I frequently become excited upon seeing a hairstreak at a distance . . . only to exclaim, `it is just a Gray' upon a closer look."[10]

"Just a Gray" is so commonplace that it is easy to become complacent about its striking beauty. "Gray" conjures dingy and dismal images, but the crisp, clear gray of this butterfly sparkles. Accented with graphic black-and-white lines and splashed with bright dots of orange, its background color is purely gray, without a hint of brown—a color trait that separates it from all other Alabama hairstreaks.

Requiring little more than plants and sunlight, Gray Hairstreaks occur in pastures, prairies, parks, and pine savannas. Scrubs, sandhills, flatwoods, coastlines, roadsides, and residential gardens also provide homes. Broods are widely overlapping, so Gray Hairstreaks seem to be around all the time.

Gray Hairstreak on Butterfly Milkweed

Gray Hairstreak
caterpillars exhibit
many color forms

Yet in spite of their pervasiveness, within these common habitats and broad time frames, only a few Gray Hairstreaks are typically encountered at any given site.

The Gray Hairstreaks' eclectic traits extend to caterpillar food preferences. Many hairstreaks are host-plant specialists, but Grays are known to choose host plants from at least thirty different families. Legumes and mallows are favorites, but the list reads like a horticultural encyclopedia and includes hops, hawthorns, corn, oaks, strawberries, hibiscus, lantanas, crotons, hickories, milkweeds, lupines, garden beans, partridge-peas, clovers, vetches, and cow-peas. When cotton was king in Alabama, Gray Hairstreaks made themselves at home in the fields, earning the nickname "cotton borer." Regardless of host-plant choice, larvae drill into buds and hollow out protein-rich interiors. Flowers and fruits are also consumed. Since caterpillar color changes according to diet, their hues wander all over the color map.

The distinguished lepidopterist Thomas Emmel once weighed in on the widespread attributes of the Gray Hairstreak. In his considered opinion (excluding the Monarch), the Gray Hairstreak most deserves the title of U.S. National Butterfly.[11]

Gray Hairstreak chrysalid in leaf litter

Basking female and male Gray Hairstreaks (note male's orange abdomen)

White-M Hairstreak *Parrhasius m-album*

White-M Hairstreaks look plain and brown when placidly nectaring. Although they sport a zigzag white M (or W) line on gray-brown wings, their coloring is subdued and mousy—until they fly. Then they transform into flashes of intense, electrifying blue. Their underwings are ordinary, but their upper surface is covered with light-reflecting scales that create structural, metallic brilliance.

These larger-than-average hairstreaks fly throughout much of the year, but are seldom seen in great numbers. Perhaps White-Ms seem scarce because giant white oaks and live oaks are their primary caterpillar hosts, ensuring that much of their time is spent high in oak canopies. When nearby spring-and-summer-flowering trees are covered with blossoms, White-Ms have little reason to descend to the ground, but during late summer and fall, they are drawn to seasonal wildflowers and may be observed intently nectaring at goldenrods, snakeroots, and thoroughworts.

White-M caterpillars cope with bitter tannins that deter many would-be oak eaters, but they eat only new plant growth, forcing their mothers to seek velvety red, barely unfurling leaves for egg placement. Spring butterflies have no problem finding fresh foliage, since entire trees are in the process of renewal. Subsequent generations must depend on intermittent growth flushes caused by storms, insect damage, or deer browsing to meet their nursery requirements. White-M caterpillars and the fresh oak leaves they ingest are often suffused with rosy hues. The addition of downy white hairs and a flattened, rounded shape results in caterpillar camouflage that is incredibly cryptic.

White-M Hairstreaks are found throughout Alabama along woodland edges which meet host and nectar requirements. Always a welcome discovery, they are easily overlooked until a quick flash of blue alerts onlookers to their presence.

White-M Hairstreak nectaring on Common White Snakeroot

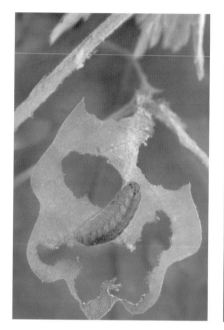

White-M Hairstreak
caterpillars exhibit
many color variations

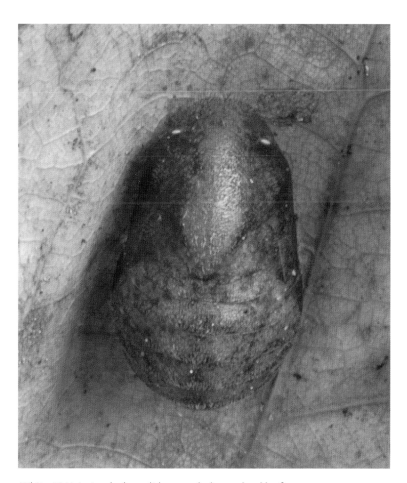

White-M Hairstreak chrysalid concealed on a dead leaf

Early Hairstreak *Erora laeta*

On April 29, 2004, a local lepidopterist found one Early Hairstreak in Alabama. The event was calendar-worthy, for it may be the only documented discovery of this uncommon insect in the state.

Early Hairstreaks are among the Southeast's most rarely encountered butterflies—whether they are actually rare is unknown. They resemble Red-Banded Hairstreaks, but minty-green wings set them apart. Females display iridescent blue dorsal wings in flight, while males are dark charcoal gray above. Both sexes are known to frequent damp soil. They also nectar from flowers that include daisy fleabanes and milkweeds. American Beech trees are believed to be their favorite hosts, and they presumably spend most of their time high in the beech canopy.

Early Hairstreak caterpillars eat developing beech fruits, and females often oviposit on these fruits rather than leaves or twigs. Green or rusty-brown larvae are marked with red splotches. Chrysalides are presumably the overwintering form. At least two broods occur during the year. Because of their caterpillars' food preferences, only mature beech forests provide suitable Early Hairstreak habitat. Beechnut production fluctuates, and Early Hairstreak populations may fluctuate accordingly.

Encounters with Early Hairstreaks are the stuff of legends in the lepidopteran world. Anecdotally, they have been encountered in large numbers, only to disappear the following day. One adventurous park ranger climbed an oak tree in search of another hairstreak and found an Early staring back at him. As for the 2004 sighting in Alabama, it reads like a familiar story. That day, following a windy, rainy night, Red-Banded Hairstreaks seemed to be everywhere. One turned out to be an Early—perhaps blown down from its canopy perch by the preceding storm. A return visit the following day found only Red-Bandeds. In spite of years of searching, the site has not yielded another Early Hairstreak.

Early Hairstreak nectaring on a daisy fleabane (photo by Will Cook)

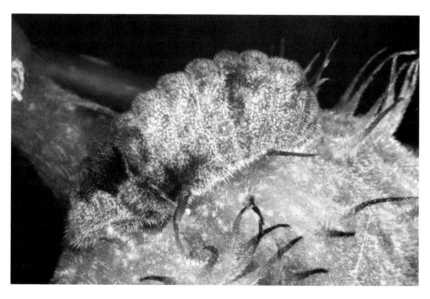

Early Hairstreak caterpillar on American Beech fruit (photo by Tom Allen)

Eastern Pygmy-Blue *Brephidium isopthalma*

Eastern Pygmy-Blues are Alabama's smallest butterflies. From tip to tip, their wingspan extends only half an inch. While their size earns pygmy designation, these "blues" are primarily brown butterflies. In their case, "blue" refers to classification rather than color because they belong to the group of small, gossamer-winged butterflies collectively known as the blues.

Eastern Pygmy-Blues flutter only inches above low-growing plants, often oblivious to observers and completely immersed in their Lilliputian world. They are tiny but tough, adapting to incredibly harsh coastal and salt marsh environments. They endure ocean winds and salt spray so that their caterpillars may feed on glassworts: tough, succulent plants that thrive in saline environments. Eggs are deposited on fleshy stems or among small, scaly leaves. Caterpillars, less than one-half inch long when completely mature, are highly camouflaged. They are identical in color to their host plants, sometimes exhibiting the same rosy flush that suffuses glasswort stems in sunny sites. Even their flattened, slug-like shapes closely resemble knobby emergences of new plant growth.

The easiest way to find cryptic pygmy-blue caterpillars is to look for gatherings of ants. Like many other blue and hairstreak larvae, they engage in mutually rewarding associations with ants called myrmecophily. In this arrangement, certain ant species aggressively defend caterpillars from parasitic flies and predatory wasps. In return, caterpillars secrete a sweet liquid reward when ants stroke special glands (Newcomer's organs) located within their abdomens. One tiny caterpillar may be tended by several even tinier ants. The guardians are so intent on protecting their prize that, regardless of size, they will attack any perceived threat—including a curious lepidopterist's probing finger.

Left: Eastern Pygmy-Blue perching on glasswort

Below left: Eastern Pygmy-Blue caterpillar attended by an ant

Below right: Eastern Pygmy-Blue basking on glasswort

Eastern Tailed-Blue *Cupido comyntas*

Eastern Tailed-Blues seem to be hairstreak impersonators. Rubbing their hindwings methodically back and forth in typical hairstreak fashion, they even sport tiny, fragile tails—the only members of their tailed subgroup in our region. With gray upper surfaces and orange spots, female Eastern Tailed-Blues are reminiscent of Gray Hairstreaks, with whom they sometimes share host plants. Ventrally, male Eastern Tailed-Blues share some resemblance, but their upper surfaces are brilliant blue, a characteristic they often flaunt by basking with partially open wings.

Throughout most of the state, Eastern Tailed-Blues are familiar sights in fields, pastures, roadsides, and other open, sunny areas. Males congregate in groups to seek nutrients from damp soil, and both sexes are attracted to low-growing flowers. Their small proboscises can only extend into short-tubed blossoms, so clovers, mints, and asters are frequent choices.

In addition to accessible nectar sources, the Eastern Tailed-Blue's habitat must also include larval food, and an assortment of legumes—vetches, clovers, and lespedezas—fits the bill. Like their fellow blues, Eastern Tailed-Blue caterpillars are primarily bud and flower eaters, and they are often colored like the blossoms they ingest. Many generations occur, and populations build as summer progresses. When warm weather ends and days become shorter, caterpillars prepare to spend winter months in diapause, sometimes tucked within a seedpod.

Weak and fluttery in flight, Eastern Tailed-Blues stay close to the ground where they barely seem to clear the tops of low-growing groundcover. They are often present in large numbers, but are easily overlooked because of their tiny size and ground-hugging tendencies.

Eastern Tailed-Blue on Swamp Milkweed

Above: Basking Eastern Tailed-Blue female

Left: Basking Eastern Tailed-Blue male

Eastern Tailed-Blue caterpillar on Virginia Goat's-Rue

Spring Azure *Celastrina ladon*

It is blue-butterfly day here in spring,
And with these sky-flakes down in flurry on flurry
There is more unmixed color on the wing
Than flowers will show for days unless they hurry.[12]

Spring Azures are the "sky-flakes" of Robert Frost's poem, "Blue-Butterfly Day." These tiny, violet-blue butterflies appear on warm spring days, "flurry on flurry" in search of mates, nectar, and ovipositing sites.

Spring Azures are woodland butterflies, and they often spiral around Flowering Dogwood, a familiar component of many Alabama forests and a favorite host plant. Females carefully deposit several disc-shaped, blue-green eggs within clusters of the tiny yellow "true" flowers located in the center of familiar white dogwood bracts. Larvae eat developing buds and flowers, boring holes to reach protein-rich pollen grains. In both color and texture, caterpillars blend perfectly with the floral bunch. Dogwoods of all types serve as cafeterias for adults as well as caterpillars since Spring Azures often nectar from their small individual flowers.

The sky-flakes do not spend all their time in the dogwood canopy. Males frequently visit damp earth where they form large puddle clubs. Tanking-up sessions must be quick, because Spring Azures are short-lived butterflies. They typically emerge, mate, reproduce, and die within a span of only four or five days.

We now know that "spring" azure is an accurate name, but for years, these tiny blues were thought to produce many generations that flew all the way through fall. In reality, Spring Azures are univoltine, generating but one brood, while a multibrooded sister species, Summer Azure, follows. By early summer, Spring Azure chrysalides rest in leaf litter where they will spend the winter waiting for lengthening days and warmer weather to signal the arrival of another "blue-butterfly day."

Above: Spring Azure on Flowering Dogwood

Left: Caterpillar curved around base of "true" dogwood flowers

Summer Azure on a daisy fleabane

Summary Azure *Celastrina neglecta*

Summer Azures typically take up where Spring Azures leave off. Near the end of their more violet-hued cousins' early spring flight, large, pale-blue Summer Azures take to the sky and fill the azure niche during summer and fall. Throughout most of the summer, they are the only azures flying. More broadly adapted than any of their celastrina cousins, they venture farther from the woods and utilize a wider variety of host plants.

Summer Azures are multibrooded, and females select a variety of flowering plants for egg laying. All typically produce tight flower clusters, and ovipositing mothers tuck thin, platelet-shaped eggs among developing buds. Swamp Dogwood and Sourwood are early season host examples, while late-summer and fall representatives include wingstems and ticktrefoils. Caterpillar color and pattern closely match their floral food. Small larvae bore holes and squeeze into buds in order to eat the nutritious interiors, completely hiding themselves from predators. Larger caterpillars are often tended by ants, which aggressively defend them against attacks. In return, caterpillars reward their protectors with sweet liquid that they excrete from special abdominal glands called Newcomer's organs.

The Latin species name, *neglecta,* is appropriate for these primarily summer-flying butterflies. For more than one hundred years, Summer Azures were overlooked as a species—considered only a seasonal form of Spring Azure. Not until 1995 were the Spring Azure and the Summer Azure recognized as completely separate entities. And they still merit taxonomic attention as evidence mounts that *Summer* Azures sometimes produce a *spring* brood.

Summer Azure caterpillar on Common New Jersey-Tea

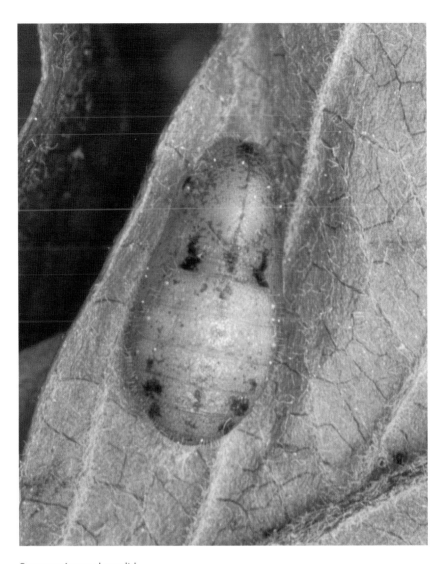

Summer Azure chrysalid

Appalachian Azure *Celastrina neglectamajor*

Appalachian Azures range into Alabama along with their namesake mountains. Designated a species only since 1984, they were previously lost within the vast, multigenerational Spring Azure complex. Lepidopterists now know that Appalachian Azures produce only one brood each year, which usually emerges after "true" Spring Azures begin to fly, but before the bulk of Summer Azures leave their chrysalides. Appalachians are normally the largest, palest butterflies of the bunch. Unfortunately, overlaps in timing and variations in size often make positive identification difficult. The most reliable indicator is not a field mark but proximity of a specific plant, for Appalachian Azures seldom wander far from their sole host, Common Black-Cohosh.

Appalachian Azures and their signature plant are found on shady, moist hillsides within mountain cove forests. The butterflies may be difficult to

Appalachian Azure on Wild Geranium

identify, but when in bloom, their plants are not. Tall spires rise as much as three feet above leaves and bear petal-less, frothy white flowers. Wiry black stems support short-stalked, bead-shaped buds—and buds are all-important for Appalachian Azures. Females oviposit on early bud structures that look more like miniature corncobs than the candle-like stalks they will become. They typically distribute several eggs on one plant. Caterpillars enthusiastically bore into bud balls, hollowing out nutritious interiors. Because of their blossoms' fragility and lengthy bloom time, black-cohosh flower stalks seldom appear pristinely white. Withered brown blooms are often found near the bottom of the stem along with new, unsullied flowers and buds nearer the top, but Appalachian Azure caterpillars have the color bases covered. Some are snowy white and blend perfectly with freshly opened flowers. Others are reddish-brown and appear to be discolored bits of flower detritus. In addition, several ants are almost always in attendance, "milking" caterpillars

Basking female Appalachian Azure

for sugary secretions and challenging any creature that might interfere with their health and welfare.

Appalachian Azures stay close to their caterpillar nursery patches. They nectar on nearby wildflowers, but are most commonly encountered sipping from damp soil along stream banks or mountain trails. Seen in company with other azures, their larger size is an identity clue, with supporting evidence offered by the presence of downy caterpillars on nearby black-cohosh spires.

Above: Appalachian Azure eggs and early instar caterpillar on immature Common Black-Cohosh flower stalk

Left: Female Appalachian Azure ovipositing on Common Black-Cohosh

Late instar Appalachian
Azure caterpillars (tend-
ed by ants) displaying
different color forms

Silvery Blue *Glaucopsyche lygdamus*

Silvery Blues are a study in graphic design. Bold, black-centered circles accent subdued gray underwings: in contrast, upper surfaces feature black-outlined, shiny sapphire surfaces. Female coloring appears tarnished and heavily edged with black, but male wings are spectacular, reflecting bright metallic blue. Fortunately for appreciative observers, they often display their namesake upperwings while basking to catch warm rays on cool spring days.

   Silvery Blues are most likely to occur in small colonies in Alabama's northeastern mountains, although historical records indicate that they may occupy more southern areas as well. They are habitat specialists, and their one and only flight is synchronized with the springtime bloom of their favored host plant, Carolina Vetch. A small, delicate legume, this trailing vine clamors sporadically about rocky woodlands. Silvery Blues nectar from its lavender-white, butterfly-shaped flowers, and they oviposit on its tightly curled bud formations. Downy green caterpillars eat buds, flowers, and, occasionally, young leaves, which their shape and color closely resemble. Ants are often

Silvery Blue basking on Carolina Vetch

in attendance, offering protection from parasitic tormentors in return for the caterpillars' sweet secretions. Most of the year is spent in pupal form, and small brown chrysalides await spring's return in nearby leaf litter.

At least two subspecies of Silvery Blue fly in the eastern United States, and several more occur in the West. In addition to Carolina Vetch, the caterpillars of the northeastern subspecies, sometimes called "Northern" Silvery Blue, reportedly accept Purple Crown-Vetch as host material. An introduced, invasive legume widely planted for erosion control, this crown-vetch covers pastures, abandoned fields, and even wooded roadsides. Northern Silvery Blues have responded accordingly, extending their southern range at a rate of approximately six miles per year. Whether our southern Appalachian-based Silvery Blue subspecies will adapt to Purple Crown-Vetch use is uncertain, but currently these butterflies remain known only from very localized populations. Even in host-filled habitat, their presence is far from guaranteed. The best way to find a Silvery Blue colony in Alabama is to locate a patch of Carolina Vetch and hope that when its flowers appear in early spring, tiny blue butterflies visit them.

Well-concealed caterpillar
on Carolina Vetch

Metalmarks
The Riodinidae

The Metalmarks or riodinids are named for glittering metallic markings that embellish their wings. These tiny butterflies often have wingspans of an inch or less, and the majority of their family members inhabit the tropics where they display dazzling colors and bizarre shapes. North American Metalmarks are considered plain in comparison, although when viewing their silvery-glinted orange wings, "plain" is not the word that comes to mind.

Metalmarks are habitat specialists and seldom stray from host-plant patches. Unlike most butterflies, they often perch with open wings, sometimes on the undersides of leaves. Their eggs resemble miniature sea urchins and their caterpillars are covered with long pale hairs. Metalmarks spend the winter as larvae. Chrysalides are often hairy and are usually attached with silk to the host plant or nearby ground litter.

Two metalmark species occur within the eastern seaboard, but Little Metalmark is Alabama's sole riodinid representative.

Little Metalmark on Savannah Sunflower

Little Metalmark *Calephelis virginiensis*

Finding a colony of Little Metalmarks is like finding a scattering of tiny jewels. Reminiscent of small moths, they are low flying, sedentary, and easy to overlook—until their minute metallic scales glint and glimmer in the sun. Then they are gloriously beautiful and instantly recognizable.

Horrid Thistle is typically designated as Little Metalmark's primary larval host, but we discovered that in Alabama's Coastal Plain, they select Vanilla-Leaf. Also called Deer Tongue, this odd plant develops a basal rosette of long leathery leaves that when crushed exude the scent of vanilla. It forms loose colonies within pinelands, savannas, and even pitcher plant bogs. Second-year plants produce tall, flowering stalks topped with flat clusters of lavender blossoms, but Little Metalmarks prefer young leaves and often choose nonflowering, first-season rosettes for egg laying. Caterpillars are peculiar creatures whose wispy white hairs look backcombed. They chew skeletonized windowpanes into leaves, an eating pattern that is distinctive and easy to spot. Chrysalides are often attached to the undersides of host leaves. Lar-

Little Metalmark basking on a goldentop

Caterpillar on Vanilla-Leaf

Caterpillar with Vanilla-Leaf's skeletonized leaves

val hairs are included in their formation, resulting in the appearance of unkempt fur balls. Several generations are produced throughout the year, but Little Metalmarks are tightly brooded, so significant gaps may exist between flights.

Metalmarks representing every color in the rainbow flit through the tropics, but in temperate Alabama, the Little Metalmark is our sole riodinid. Yellow daisy-shaped flowers are favorite nectar sources, and these tiny gem-like butterflies often sit with wings completely outstretched as they sip, dazzling observers who get close enough for a good look.

Little Metalmark nectaring on a thoroughwort

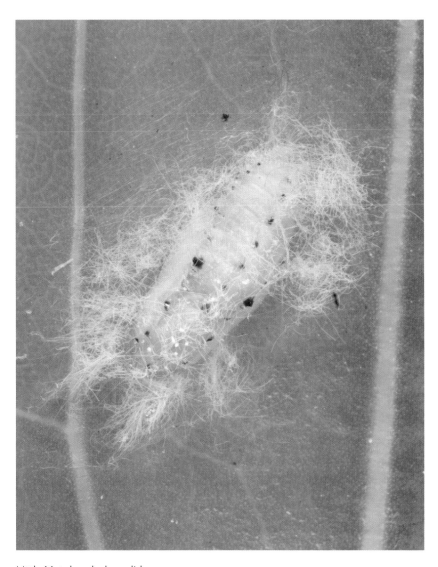

Little Metalmark chrysalid

A Common Wood Nymph displays prominent false eyes.

Brushfoots
The Nymphalidae

Brushfoots are named for their small, furry forelegs. So reduced in size that these butterflies often appear to be four-legged, they are useless for walking, but function as sensors. These stunted appendages are one of the only characteristics that unify the widely diverse Nymphalid family. Within it are the longest-lived butterflies and the farthest travelers. Many of its members are extremely colorful but others are drab. There are nectar drinkers, carrion sippers, and pollen eaters. Some lay their eggs singly; others precariously stack them; still others lay them in great clusters. Their caterpillars eat the leaves of trees, herbaceous plants, and even grasses. Some are mimics, and others are highly camouflaged, while some flaunt their toxicity. A few stick close to their host plants, but others travel great distances, and one even migrates.

Many groups currently considered to be Nymphalid subfamilies or tribes were once classified as completely separate families. Even now, their differences are so great that they warrant their own descriptions.

The Snouts are an ancient group, and only one species occurs in our region. Thickened palps look like a beak or snout. Most snouts are orange and brown, and their forewing tips are square. They are strong fliers, and some engage in mass migrations (although Alabama's snouts do not). Caterpillars feed on hackberry trees.

The Milkweed Butterflies (or *Danaids*) are large insects that have no frost tolerance in any stage of their life cycle. Typically toxic, caterpillars sequester cardiac glycosides for their milkweed hosts. Warning coloration in both larval and adult stages advertises their toxicity. Males possess abdominal hairpencils and hindwing scent patches that are used in courtship. Danaids have tough bodies, enabling them to survive attacks by adventurous or uneducated predators. They are avid nectarers.

The Admirals are large, showy butterflies that tend to be mimics. They often gain nourishment from nonfloral sources but occasionally visit flowers. Flight typically alternates several wing beats with short, open-winged glides. Males perch to find females. They overwinter as mid-stage caterpillars.

Abundant in the tropics, the Longwings (or *Heliconians*) derive strong chemical toxins from their passion-flower host plants and are unpalatable in all developmental forms. They exhibit elongated wings, slender bodies, large eyes, and long antennae. Sometimes considered a northern version of the Longwings, the Fritillaries are typically large and orange. Violets are their common caterpillar hosts. The Greater Fritillaries are univoltine and overwinter as first instar larvae.

Like the broad family of Brushfoots from which it borrows its common name, the group known as the Typical Brushfoots is extremely diverse. Buckeyes are known for their showy eyespots. Anglewings are dorsally camouflaged. Checkerspots and crescents display shades of black and orange. Generally, the Typical Brushfoots overwinter as adults.

Emperors and Leafwings primarily feed at sap flows, rotting fruit, and carrion. They rarely visit flowers. Both groups aggressively defend territories, and males are "perchers." Caterpillars are typically tapered at both ends. Emperor caterpillars have horned heads and tend to feed communally, while Leafwing larvae are solitary feeders.

The Satyrs are the exception to many Nymphalid family rules. Their colors are drab and muted while most Brushfoots are brightly colored. Their caterpillars eat grass and sedges, which are monocotyledons—all other Nymphalid larvae eat dicotyledons. Short proboscises prevent satyrs from nectaring at deep-tubed flowers, so they rely on nonfloral energy sources. Their forewings contain a swelling that performs a rudimentary auditory function. Males also have scent patches, which they use in courtship. Satyr flight is typically bouncy and unpredictable.

Gulf Fritillary nectaring on Butterfly Milkweed

American Snout *Libytheana carinenta*

No butterfly in North America has a "snout" like this one. Seen in flight, the American Snout's identity may be in question. But viewed at rest, there is no mistaking its silhouette for any other. The adaptive purpose of these remarkable elongated mouthparts (or "palps") has long been questioned. Perhaps it simply enables the butterfly to impersonate a dry leaf complete with upturned stem or petiole, an effect that is enhanced by the forward placement of its antennae.

Snouts have a long relationship with hackberries, their sole host plants. Thirty-million-year-old fossils show ancient snouts (complete with palps) preserved alongside ancient hackberries. Present-day females flutter at branch tips before depositing single eggs amid crinkled new leaves. Caterpillars depend on camouflage for protection, but assume a defensive, sphinx-like position when disturbed or alarmed. Although they are often described as mimicking furled foliage, a head-on view reveals a tiny snake-like visage.

Like their larvae, adults employ camouflage and startle tactics to aid in defense against vertebrate predators. Perched snouts resemble dead leaves. Simply closing and compressing their wings results in a virtual disappearing act. However, by quickly raising their forewings, previously invisible butterflies flash attackers with distracting patches of orange.

Snouts are only occasionally encountered at flowers, but they avidly seek salts and minerals by puddling. Males frequently seek these same substances on perspiring skin, where their curious, prehistoric countenances can be closely admired.

Perched American Snout

Caterpillar on a hackberry

Defensive American Snout caterpillar exhibiting false eyespots

Basking American Snout

American Snout nectaring on Tall Thoroughwort

Monarch *Danaus plexippus*

Monarchs are the most celebrated and well-known butterflies in North America. They are familiar residents of Alabama and occur in every county. Many schoolchildren recognize their distinctive colors and can relate their life stories, yet, because of the Monarchs' migratory patterns, most Alabamians actually encounter them only in fall and spring when thousands pass through the state on their way to and from their Mexican wintering grounds.

Highly traveled Monarchs are famous for their reliance on poisonous host plants called milkweeds. These well-protected plants contain cardenolides and cardiac glycosides, bitter-tasting chemicals that cause congestive heart failure in vertebrates. Monarch caterpillars not only devour these toxins, but also stockpile them within their bodies and retain them through metamorphosis. Birds vomit when they ingest chemical-filled larvae and/or adults and

Monarch on a blazing-star

quickly learn to avoid brightly striped caterpillars and large orange and black butterflies. But not all milkweeds are created equal. Some contain few if any cardenolides, and Monarch caterpillars that eat these species are not well protected. Others are so high in chemical content that caterpillars "bleed" leaves by chewing partially through leaf petioles, allowing some of the toxic milky latex to drain away. Butterfly Milkweed is on the lower end of the poison scale, while Swamp Milkweed ranks higher. Given a choice, female Monarchs choose milkweeds that fall in the middle range. As long as enough predators eat truly toxic butterflies to believe that all are distasteful, the system works.

In addition to their remarkable host-plant adaptability, Monarchs have also solved the problem of cold intolerance. They simply migrate to warmer climates—a feat that involves flying thousands of miles and circumnavigating across a continent. The journey begins in fall, when Monarchs begin to fly south from their northernmost homes in Canada. Large numbers follow the Appalachian Mountain range, and these migrants eventually stream through Alabama, adding local butterflies to their numbers. Many make it to the Alabama coast where, to the delight of visitors and residents, they roost communally on trees and shrubs before heading across the Gulf or continuing their southward journey via Texas.

Once in the high mountains of central Mexico, Monarchs cling by the millions to fir branches, occasionally nectaring on warm days, but primarily living off stored fat reserves. Everything is geared toward basic survival, so reproduction is delayed until spring. When lengthening days signal spring's imminent arrival, mating occurs, and the tattered travelers begin the trip home. Monarchs typically reach Alabama by March, nectaring at spring flowers, and depositing eggs on every available milkweed patch. Although no individual butterfly completes the entire journey, subsequent generations keep moving north toward Canada, leaving only small populations in residence.

Monarch butterflies are the official state insect of Alabama, an honor they also hold in five other states. Monarchs tickle our fancies and capture our imaginations, perhaps because—from poison-eating caterpillar to continent-navigating butterfly—they seem to routinely accomplish the impossible.

Monarch caterpillar on Butterfly Milkweed

Monarch chrysalid

Communal Monarch roost on Dauphin Island during fall migration

Male Monarchs on Groundsel-Tree

Queen (male) nectaring on Groundsel-Tree

Queen *Danaus gilippus*

Queens are milkweed butterflies. They are similar in appearance to the infamous milkweed butterfly, the Monarch, but parts of their lifestyle differ dramatically. They lack the Monarch's wanderlust and do not engage in its massive annual migrations. Queens are year-round residents only in the Deep South, moving up the coast as warm weather and host-plant distribution permit. In Alabama, they are uncommon summer and fall residents and seldom venture past coastal counties.

Queens fly in sunny, maritime environments, such as tidal marshes, shrub thickets, and dunes. Although many types of milkweed satisfy host-plant requirements, on Dauphin Island we have found them associated with Gulf Coast Swallow-Wort, a sprawling vine whose crown-shaped flowers, oozing latex, and fluffy white seeds suggest its Milkweed family origins. Swallow-worts contain toxic cardiac glycosides, which Queen caterpillars (like Monarchs) safely sequester and retain into adulthood. They derive protection from vertebrate predators who find the chemicals distasteful and sickening, and both larvae and adults advertise their bad taste with warning coloration. Like Monarch caterpillars, Queen larvae brandish fleshy filaments at both head and tail ends, but Queens also add a pair in the middle.

Differentiating Queens from Monarchs is not difficult, and neither is distinguishing male from female Queens. Dark scent patches dot male hindwings and disperse an alluring pheromone called danaidone that induces females to mate. Synthesized from plants containing poisonous pyrrolizidine alkaloids (PAs), male Queens store danaidone in their wing patches. In addition to these pheromone glands, bristly structures called hairpencils are contained within male abdomens. By extruding their hairpencils and raking them over the scent patches, male butterflies access danaidone and then apply it to female antennae. The pheromone convinces a female Queen to mate, and during the process, it is transferred into her body with the sperm packet. Its poisonous properties are subsequently incorporated into her eggs. Because the production of danaidone is crucial to the courtship process, suit-

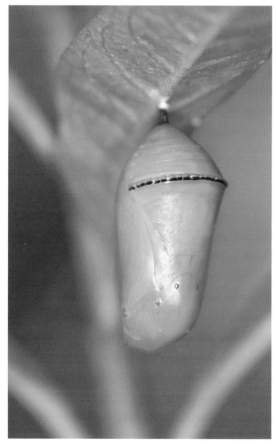

Above: Queen caterpillar on Gulf Coast Swallow-Wort

Left: Queen chrysalid

Queen male displaying a hairpencil

able Queen habitat must contain PA-producing plants like thoroughworts, rattleboxes, heliotropes, and groundsels. Male Queens not only drink from their flowers but also probe for PA remnants on dried stems and spent blossoms.

To the delight of south Alabama butterfly gardeners, Queens nectar from many additional flowers, including milkweeds, beggarticks, and cultivated lantana. Their slow, gliding flight is reminiscent of the Monarchs' flight, and their caterpillars often share the same host plants. Although Queens are not as famous as their cousins, their life history is equally fascinating, if not as far-flung.

Queen male probing for pyrrolizidine alkaloids on dried thoroughworts

Queen visiting beggarticks

Red-Spotted Purple *Limenitis arthemis astyanax*

Red-Spotted Purples are consummate mimics. These black and blue butterflies strongly resemble Pipevine Swallowtails, so it is surprising to learn that Red-Spotted Purples are very closely related to Viceroys: orange and black butterflies that strongly resemble Monarchs. Although the cousins display dramatically different coloring, their shapes are virtually identical. Family ties are most evident in early developmental stages, where egg, larva, and pupa are almost indistinguishable.

Red-Spotted Purples typically choose host plants from the Rose family, and Black Cherry is a common favorite. Females place single, pitted white eggs on leaf tips. From the beginning, Red-Spotted Purple caterpillars are masters in the art of self-protection. They mimic feces and never discard that guise. In addition to their disgusting coloration, they also bear barbed antennae and bristly bumps (although they are not as spiny as Viceroy larvae). First

Red-Spotted Purple on a thoroughwort

Early instar caterpillar with frass chain

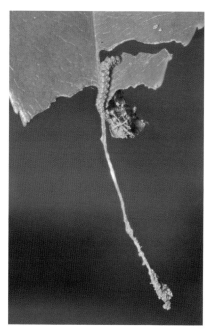

Early instar caterpillar with leaf ball

Hibernaculum

and second instar caterpillars string their dung pellets onto the ends of leaf midribs and avoid ants and other walking predators by resting at the end of the frass chain. They also devise distracting balls of chewed leaf morsels and more dung, which they hang near the eaten portion of their leaf. The lightweight structures wave in the wind and may draw attention away from their tiny architects. Larger instars rest on branches unless actively consuming leaves. Late-season, partially grown caterpillars construct tightly shaped leaf tubes called hibernacula in which they spend the winter. These small enclosures are tightly tied to tree branches, looking like nothing more than clinging, dead leaves. When fresh foliage emerges in spring, Red-Spotted Purple caterpillars also emerge from their chambers and complete larval development. They dangle upside down from a twig to form their oddly shaped, cryptically colored chrysalides.

Red-Spotted Purples sip from overly ripe fruit, dung, and decaying matter. They are also avid puddlers and are frequently encountered along woodland trails and roads, where inquiring minds often wonder, "Why aren't they called Orange-Spotted Blues?"

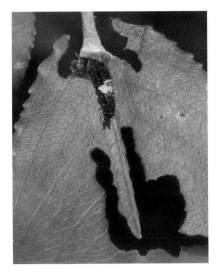 

Above left: Mid-instar Red-Spotted Purple caterpillar beginning to construct hibernaculum

Above right: Red-Spotted Purple caterpillar beginning its pupal transformation

Above: Red-Spotted Purple
on Butterfly Milkweed

Left: Red-Spotted Purple
chrysalid

Viceroy *Limenitis archippus*

Viceroys are famous because they look like Monarchs. For years, lepidop-terists believed that avian aversion to poisonous Monarch butterflies trans-ferred to look-alike Viceroys. The copycats were presumed to benefit from the confusing similarity. But Viceroys, thought to get by only on their looks, bring a lot more to the table than orange and black wings. They have their own brand of bad-tasting nastiness acquired from phytochemical-filled host plants, primarily willows. These trees contain salicin (the bitter-tasting ingre-dient in aspirin), and although not necessarily toxic, its taste is so unpleasant that many predators avoid it as well as the insects that eat it. Not only do Viceroys benefit from looking like Monarchs, but Monarchs also benefit from looking like Viceroys.

Viceroys are found throughout Alabama wherever willows grow. Stream and riverbanks, marsh and swamp edges, and moist deciduous woodlands are all likely habitats. Males find the perfect perch, usually only a few feet

Viceroy basking on a willow

from the ground, and settle in to look for females. They are not patient suitors and frequently sally forth to patrol the territory before resuming their open-winged stance at the original roost. Females are more likely to be found within willow groves, where they search for suitable ovipositing sites.

Viceroys place their round, dimpled eggs on leaf tips, and distribute their ova singly throughout the branches. Early instar larvae take extraordinary measures to ensure their safety from predators. Not content to rely on bird-dropping disguises, they eat material near the leaf's point, leaving only the midrib. To this exposed filament, they add pellets of their own minuscule frass, gradually extending the leaf's vein with a string of excrement. Tiny larvae rest at the end of the frass chain where ambulatory predators, like ants, generally refuse to follow. In addition to this architectural achievement, Viceroy caterpillars also construct detritus balls from frass and leaf bits. These loosely formed orbs wave and wiggle with the slightest breeze and may distract predators with their eye-catching movements. When caterpillars outgrow their frass chains, they desert both balls and chains and begin to rest

Mid-instar caterpillar
with leaf ball

Viceroy in Hibernaculum

on twigs and branches. Depending on the season, some caterpillars simply eat until pupation time, but autumn's brood must perform one more construction job. Partially grown caterpillars assemble small structures called hibernacula in which they spend winter months. They chew away the bottom third of a leaf, roll the remainder into a tight tube, and then securely silk it to the tree. Entering head first into their resting chamber, diapausing larvae spend the winter dangling from a bare willow branch. When leaves appear and catkins swell, small Viceroy caterpillars emerge from their sleeping bags and resume development. Final instars retain their bird-dropping disguises,

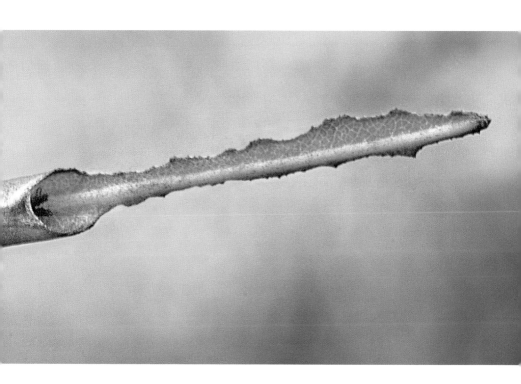

although their lumpy bodies and branched horns distinguish them from any similarly disguised swallowtail caterpillar. It is a toss up whether Viceroy chrysalides most resemble broken twigs or very large droppings.

Viceroys sail through the air with a distinctive flap and glide pattern, usually coasting with outstretched wings. This flight pattern helps to differentiate them from Monarchs, which glide with wings in V-formation. Despite these flight differences, their slightly smaller size, and an extra hindwing line, Viceroys look a lot like Monarchs. Or perhaps, Monarchs look a lot like Viceroys.

Viceroy caterpillars exhibiting defensive postures

Perching Viceroy

Gulf Fritillary nectaring on Purple-Top Vervain

Gulf Fritillary *Agraulis vanillae*

Philip Henry Gosse called it "the most splendid butterfly I had ever seen." Almost two hundred years later, the Gulf Fritillary's beauty still delights observers. Its brilliant upper surface is deep, velvety orange, veined in black, and dotted with three pearly-white spots. But as Gosse concluded, "it is in the under surface that the superlative glory of this most lovely insect is seen."[13] There, tawny ventral wings display shades of yellow and even vermillion, and large silver teardrops sparkle and flash in the sunlight. Females are slightly larger and browner than males, but they are still stunningly beautiful.

In spite of their fritillary-like color scheme, Gulf Fritillaries are not true fritillaries. They are actually classified as longwings (or heliconians). Their forewings are not as narrow as those of other longwings, but the classic shape is evident when Gulf Fritillaries bask with outstretched wings. Although many heliconian butterflies eat pollen in addition to drinking flower nectar, Gulf Fritillaries are strictly nectar sippers. Their caterpillars are more typically "longwing" and eat passion-flowers, that family's host plants.

In Alabama, two native passion-flower species play host to Gulf Fritillaries. Purple Passion-Flower (or "Maypop") is a sprawling vine that rambles

Egg on passion-flower tendril

through pastures, roadsides, and other sunny sites. Its complex purple-and-white-fringed flowers have fascinated generations of children, and its large round fruits are sometimes made into jelly. Yellow Passion-Flower is much less conspicuous and prefers shady sites where it clamors up trees and twines along the ground. Small yellow-green flowers blossom when the vine reaches sunlight. Passion-flowers vigorously defend themselves against hungry butterfly caterpillars. Their leaves contain cyanogenic glycosides, which should function as powerful deterrents, but Gulf Fritillary caterpillars adapted to their lethal attributes long ago and sequester them to use in their own defense against birds and lizards—a toxicity they advertise with shiny orange and black warning colors. Ants prey on butterfly eggs, and passion-flowers developed nectar glands at their leaf bases that attract ants to their vines by rewarding them with sweet liquid. Once again, Gulf Fritillaries adjusted: they frequently bypass passion-flower leaves to lay eggs on its curling tendrils, safely avoiding hungry ants. The arms race continues, but in spite of all their

Above: Gulf Fritillary caterpillar on Purple Passion-Flower

Opposite: Gulf Fritillary caterpillar on Yellow Passion-Flower

Gulf Fritillary chrysalid attached to asters

Gulf Fritillary (male) nectaring on a goldentop

formidable defenses, maypops are frequently eaten to the ground by voracious Gulf Fritillary caterpillars.

Gulf Fritillaries are highly adapted to their host plants, but they are not as tolerant of freezing weather, so each year the anticipation of winter pushes their populations back to the south. Massive flights occur in the fall, as northern butterflies travel through Alabama to the Gulf coast and southward into Florida. Along the way, these beautiful butterflies nectar at flowers on roadsides and in pastures, parks, and powerline right-of-ways. Gulf Fritillaries are also frequent garden visitors, where they are still often considered "the most splendid" of butterflies.

Gulf Fritillary (female) on Shoreline Sea-Purslane

Zebra Longwing *Heliconius charithonia*

Zebra Longwings are Florida visitors who sometimes put down very shallow roots in Alabama. The Sunshine State's official butterfly, they are primarily tropical insects that move north only when warm temperatures allow. At the first sign of a freeze, their population shrinks to its original boundaries. In good years, Zebra Longwings make it to Alabama's southernmost counties. They bring with them a look and a lifestyle that is like no other.

Zebra Longwings are quintessential heliconians, and their narrow elongated wing shapes and yellow-on-black striping is unmistakable. The coloration sends a warning: "Don't eat me. I taste bad." Although their caterpillars eat poisonous passion-flowers, adults do not retain these toxins. Instead, they manufacture additional poisons within their own bodies.

In a bizarre twist, Zebra Longwing butterflies are not only nectar drinkers,

Zebra Longwing on beggarticks

they are also pollen eaters. They collect protein-rich pollen grains on their proboscises, which they dissolve with regurgitated stomach enzymes before ingesting. Because of their high-protein diets, Zebra Longwings are particularly long lived: single individuals may survive as long as six months. Multiple generations roost together at night, and young adults may learn the locations of roost sites and nectar sources from older individuals.

Like all heliconians, Zebra Longwing caterpillars require a diet of passionflowers (or passifloras), a group of plants that has developed many defen-

Pollen on Zebra Longwing proboscis

sive adaptations during its evolutionary history. Regardless of the many protective punches that passifloras throw in the fight against herbivory, Zebra Longwings manage to counter with their own incredible adaptations. In spite of confusing leaf shapes, ant-attracting nectaries, faux eggs, shedding plant parts, and an array of toxic phytochemicals, Zebra Longwing caterpillars still devour their viney hosts. In Alabama, Yellow Passion-Flower is a favorite, because its ability to grow in dappled sunlight matches the Zebra Longwings' preference for shade.

Zebra Longwing caterpillars are twice protected. They sequester toxic cyanogenic glycosides from their passion-flower hosts (a fact they advertise with eye-catching black-and-white coloration), and six rows of wickedly sharp spines cover their bodies. As is the case with all North American butterfly caterpillars, spines may deter some predators, but they are harmless to human beings.

Chrysalides are outlandishly ornamented structures with their own protective adaptations. From some angles, they resemble withered leaves, but viewed straight on, they display a fierce, prickly-jawed countenance, perfect for predator intimidation. Although pupae are camouflaged and even scary, adult longwings are impervious to both guises. Able to sense which pupae contain females, male butterflies line up for the opportunity to mate. An especially lucky suitor may actually achieve copulation while the chrysalid is still intact. Further pairings are discouraged because the triumphant male gifts his mate with an aphrodisiac-reducing hormone that makes her unattractive to other suitors.

Zebra Longwings should be sought in Alabama's southern counties, particularly along forest edges that support stands of Yellow Passion-Flower. Typically found flitting slowly through dappled shade, Zebra Longwings are also commonly encountered in flower gardens. In years without hard freezes, populations may remain intact for a few months, but generally these graceful heliconian butterflies must reenter Alabama each year from the Sunshine State.

Opposite: Zebra Longwing caterpillar on Yellow Passion-Flower

Zebra Longwing chrysalid suspended from a passion-flower tendril

Zebra Longwing nectaring on a goldenrod

Variegated Fritillary *Euptoieta claudia*

Variegated Fritillaries bridge the gap between the Greater Fritillaries (or *Speyarias*) and the Longwings (or *Heliconias*), exhibiting characteristics of both groups. Most greater fritillaries have rounded orange, silver-spotted wings; produce a single yearly brood; and choose violets as their larval hosts. Longwing butterflies have narrow, elongated wing shapes; are multibrooded; and use passion-flowers as their only hosts. With their rusty-orange wings, Variegateds strongly resemble the Greater Fritillaries but are significantly smaller and lack silver spots. They do not exhibit the classic "longwing" shape but are multibrooded and their caterpillars devour the Longwings' trademark passion-flowers—but not exclusively. In true "crazy-mixed-up-kid" fashion, they also eat violets, sole hosts of the Greater Fritillaries.

Variegated Fritillaries are common residents of open, sunny areas that support nectar flowers and host plants, but they are rarely seen in large numbers. Eye-catching when nectaring, they are easily alarmed and somewhat difficult to approach. Their tawny upper surface is so striking that their more subtly hued underside is often overlooked—literally. When perched with closed wings, the Variegateds' muted markings resemble a dried leaf, a particularly useful disguise since adults live through the winter and can more easily blend with its landscape.

While Variegated Fritillary butterflies are lovely, their caterpillars and chrysalides are downright flashy. Caterpillars sport shiny orange, black, and white markings as well as wicked-looking barbed black spines. They resemble Gulf Fritillary larvae with which they often share passion-flower vines, but Gulf caterpillars lack white accents and are not as gaudy. The coloring of both species actively advertises that they are distasteful. Variegated Fritillary chrysalides are a jewel-like study in mother-of-pearl, gold, and onyx.

Although Variegated Fritillaries produce several generations each year, in much of Alabama, they are most abundant in summer and fall. They cannot withstand freezing temperatures, but by early summer these "lesser" fritillaries have recolonized the coldest spots in the state and are actively pursuing the lifestyle of taxonomic fence sitters.

Variegated Fritillary on Brazilian Vervain

Above: Variegated Fritillary caterpillar eating a violet

Opposite: Variegated Fritillary caterpillar on Purple Passion-Flower

Above: Variegated Fritillary chrysalid

Opposite: Variegated Fritillary on Fringed Bluestars

Diana Fritillary *Speyeria diana*

Diana Fritillaries pack a one-two punch. With impressive four-inch wing-spans, a male is a stunning combination of rich brown and velvety orange. Large and graceful in flight, it seems as good as it gets for a butterfly—then along comes the female, every bit as stunning in her jet black and iridescent blue. Why this color combination of daylight and dark? Male Dianas display a typical fritillary color palette, but females mimic distasteful black-and-blue Pipevine Swallowtails.

Life cycles of the opposing genders are as different as their appearances. Males emerge in late spring and early summer and begin to tank up on nectar and minerals in preparation for their soon-to-emerge mates. When females finally arrive on the scene, coupling occurs, and the male mission is accomplished. By midsummer, most are gone, but for surviving females, life is just beginning. They retreat deep into the woods for summer's duration, rest in the heat of the day, and emerge from their forested haunts only to nectar. In

Diana (male) on Butterfly Milkweed

Diana (female) on a thistle

Chrysalid webbed in leaf litter

early fall, they resume an active lifestyle and get down to the all-important business of reproduction. Crawling along the ground, females deposit eggs near patches of violets. After hatching, tiny larvae bypass food and quickly hide in ground litter to settle in for the winter. Very early the following year, as soon as temperatures rise and violet leaves sprout, the little black fuzz balls start to nibble. When spring finally arrives, their appetites are insatiable and rapid development begins. Fully mature caterpillars are corpulent. Sharp black spines erupt from orange tubercles, warning potential predators that these frightening creatures should be avoided. Pupation occurs in loosely constructed nests in leaves or leaf litter, and a few weeks later, when male butterflies emerge, the cycle begins again.

Typically expected in Alabama's northeastern mountains, Diana Fritillaries also turn up in unexpected spots and range sporadically at least as far south as Tallapoosa County. Their survival requires a complex combination of habitats that must combine open, sunny areas with nearby deciduous forests. In addition to their violet hosts, a succession of crucial, and perhaps specific, nectar plants such as milkweeds and thistles must also be accessible. An alarming rangewide decline in Diana populations over the past fifty years is reason to focus on gathering more information about this beautiful butterfly's specialist lifestyle.

Left: Diana Fritillary chrysalid attached to a violet leaf

Opposite: Final instar Diana Fritillary caterpillar eating a violet

Diana Fritillary (male) on Poke Milkweed

Diana Fritillary (female) on a thistle

Great Spangled Fritillary *Speyeria cybele*

Great Spangled Fritillaries are attention grabbers. Their three-inch wing-span, bright pumpkin color, and large silver spangles catch the eye. They frequent open sunny habitats and head for orange milkweed and purple thistle blooms, both of which not only create stunning color combinations, but also produce intensely rich nectar that helps sustain these butterflies' extended life cycle. Like all greater fritillaries, Great Spangleds are single-brooded. Males come out in early summer, usually several days earlier than their female counterparts, and are highly visible as they actively search for partners. When females emerge, mating occurs, and the male life cycle quickly runs its course. Females live on in a state of reproductive diapause, and during

Great Spangled Fritillary
on Bear's-Foot

July and August they are seldom seen as they hide in nearby woodlands. The eggs within their bodies do not mature until late summer, when females leave the forest to deposit them in the vicinity of violets. Caterpillars hatch a few weeks later, but do not eat. Instead, they hide in leaf litter near their violet hosts and immediately enter diapause. They aestivate until warm temperatures awaken them for snacks on emergent violet leaves. When spring arrives in earnest, they consume mass quantities of food, crawling along the woodland floor from one plant to the next. Barbed spines discourage meal seekers, and their first line of defense is usually to drop and roll. But caterpillars are also armed with bulb-shaped, osmeteria-like glands that emit an unpleasant musky odor. Located under the head, these brightly colored structures bulge when larvae are in protection mode. Large butterflies come from

Caterpillar
eating a violet

large caterpillars, and these fat black creatures may reach a full two inches in length. Fully grown larvae construct a loose nest of leaves and form a chrysalid within. Approximately two weeks later, the first males emerge.

Range maps often indicate that Great Spangled Fritillaries only inhabit Alabama's northeastern corner. Fortunately, these beautiful butterflies extend farther into the state, where they have caught the eyes of admirers at least as far south as the fall line.

Above: Defensive Great Spangled Fritillary caterpillar extruding bulbous orange osmeterium from below head

Opposite: Great Spangled Fritillary chrysalid

Great Spangled Fritillary on Common Milkweed

Hackberry Emperor *Asterocampa celtis*

In Alabama, chances are great that a grove of hackberry trees supports a colony of Hackberry Emperors. The trees may go unnoticed, but it is hard to overlook the rattly whirring of wings and the curious, salt-loving butterflies that often hitchhike on sweaty arms and perspiration-damp clothing. Although they may stick around a while, males are territorial and stake out particular perches, returning to the same ones again and again. The more round-winged females are not quite as social, often remaining higher in trees. Both sexes rarely nectar at flowers, preferring sap, fruit, detritus, and damp dirt instead.

Each of Alabama's three hackberry (or "celtis") species plays host to Hackberry Emperors, but Sugarberry (or Southern Hackberry) is by far the most common. Shade tolerant, it is often found in bottomlands but is equally at home in parks and suburban neighborhoods. Hackberry Emperors spread their eggs throughout the foliage of small host trees, placing them singly or in very small clusters on the undersides of young leaves. Caterpillar heads are wreathed in thorny antlers, and coupled with their thick bodies and tapered

Late instar caterpillar on a hackberry

Hackberry Emperor sipping from Autumn-Olive fruit

ends, they create distinctive silhouettes. Yellow-green stripes and dashes disguise larvae as bits of foliage, but chrysalid camouflage is incredible. It precisely duplicates the color and pattern of hackberry foliage, complete with faux leaf venation.

The season's final generation of Hackberry Emperors spends the winter as partially grown caterpillars. They protect themselves from the elements by constructing a rolled leaf shelter, silking it to a tree, and hibernating within it. Chameleon-like, larvae turn from green to brown to match their dead leaf sleeping bags and then turn green again when feeding resumes in the spring.

Highly camouflaged Hackberry Emperor chrysalid attached to a hackberry leaf

Hackberry Emperor on a cypress knee

Tawny Emperor *Asterocampa clyton*

Tawny Emperors seem virtually identical to Hackberry Emperors, so why are they almost always in the minority? Although Tawnies are usually a little brighter and "tawnier" than Hackberries, the two species are remarkably alike in size, shape, and pattern. As adults, both species feed primarily on nonflower sources such as dung, sap, and overripe fruit: as caterpillars, they only eat hackberries. Both are frequent puddlers, and both are persistent visitors to human extremities in their pursuit of salty fluids. Yet in spite of these shared characteristics, Tawny Emperors are encountered less frequently and almost always in smaller numbers.

Tawny and Hackberry Emperor caterpillars also look like twins, but their lifestyles are remarkably different. Rather than dispersing their eggs throughout the canopy, Tawnies mass them in large clusters. Females painstakingly stack pyramid-style layers of minute pale-green eggs, and their ova often number in the hundreds. The small army that hatches is able to collectively chew through tough, mature leaves, enabling Tawny Emperors to fill a niche on hackberry trees left open by many new-growth eaters, including Hackberry Emperors and American Snouts. There may be safety in numbers, but the lucky predator that discovers the congregation of caterpillars can make

Egg cluster

Tawny Emperor on fallen Trumpet-Creeper flower

quick work of its constituents. We have observed yellow jackets carrying off caterpillar after caterpillar from a Tawny Emperor cluster. Assuming they escape mass annihilation, larvae remain together through three instars, laying down trails of silk as they move from leaf to leaf. Smaller groups form when

Left: Tawny Emperor caterpillars emerging from eggs

Below: Tawny Emperor caterpillars skeletonizing hackberry leaves

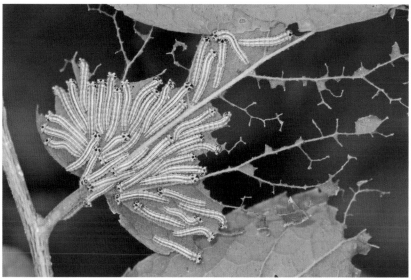

Tawny Emperor caterpillars (several instars) on hackberry leaves

Left: Prepupal phase Tawny Emperor caterpillar in silked hackberry leaf

Below: Highly camouflaged Tawny Emperor chrysalid on far right hackberry leaf

hackberry leaves can no longer hold them in bulk, but even late-season caterpillars that must overwinter remain together. Collectively they construct a shelter of silked leaves that they tie to a branch tip. There they spend the winter in diapause, having changed color to become as brown as the dead leaves that surround them. Final instar larvae become more solitary. At maturity, each caterpillar attaches itself to the underside of a hackberry leaf and forms a chrysalid that perfectly matches hackberry foliage in color and pattern.

Tawny Emperors are found wherever hackberry trees (and Hackberry Emperors) abound. In fact, they are almost never encountered outside the company of their close cousins. For unknown reasons, the reverse is not true.

Tawny Emperor basking on a hackberry

American Lady on Stiff Tickseed

American Lady *Vanessa virginiensis*

The American Lady is often considered the *other* lady. Its more famous, look-alike cousin, the Painted Lady, has taken American popular culture by storm through the marketing of caterpillar-rearing kits, and its migratory exploits are legendary. The American Lady seems to pale in comparison. Even Philip Henry Gosse noted, "It is so much like the Painted Lady . . . that one would be tempted to think it the same."[14] Yet the American Lady was once commonly called the "Painted Beauty" and is the more striking of the two species. Its cobwebbed hindwing pattern is precise and clearly defined, and its two large eyespots are large and dramatic—Painted Lady butterflies exhibit only four or five small, obscure spots against a mottled background. Although the Painted Lady is better known, it is not cold tolerant, and it must recolonize Alabama every year, but the American Lady maintains constant residence.

American Ladies are habitat generalists, living almost anywhere as long as their host plants, which include pussytoes and cudweeds, are nearby. These low-growing, gray-leaved "everlastings" are so widespread and weedy that American Ladies can range from dunes and savannas to powerline clearings and urban yards. Plantain-Leaf Pussytoes is a mat-forming, fuzzy-flowered perennial and an American Lady favorite. Female ladies carefully work their abdomens deep within felt-like leaf fuzz to deposit single eggs. Tiny caterpillars make use of the plant hairs to make small nests, and older larvae arrange leaves, flower heads, and detritus to form tight shelters. Several structures may be built as hungry crawlers move from one small plant to another. Only the inside layers of leaves are eaten, allowing the occupant to remain completely hidden. Leafy nests keep them out of sight, but caterpillars are also armed with branching spines that aid in defense against predation.

American Ladies sip nectar from many different plant species. Members of the Aster family are favorites, but in the spring, flowering plums may find these butterflies among their visitors. Although American Ladies are Alabama's most common *Vanessa* species, careful observers may note that *V. virginiensis* and *V. cardui* sometimes nectar side by side. Then a careful count of hindwing eyespots will reveal the Lady's true identity.

Left: American Lady
nest constructed in
pussytoes leaves

Below: American Lady
on Stiff Tickseed

Opposite: Final instar
American Lady
caterpillar on pussytoes

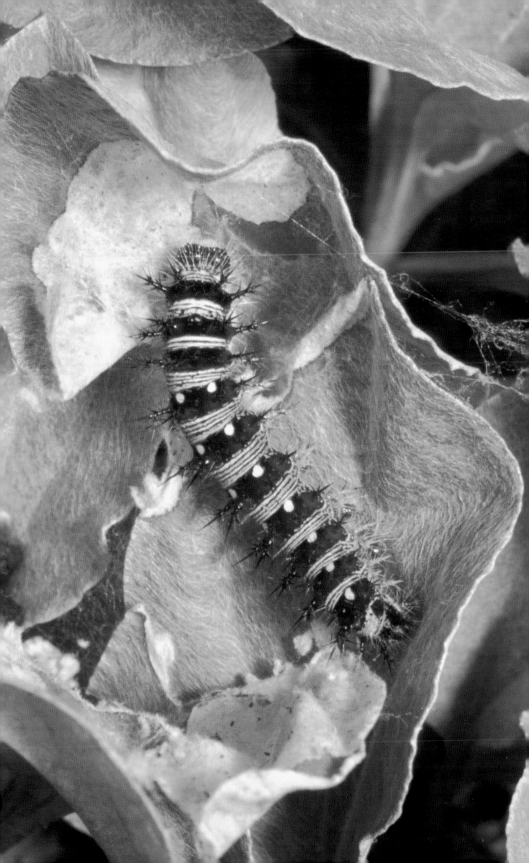

Painted Lady *Vanessa cardui*

Painted Ladies are supremely adaptable. They are at home throughout the continental United States, and they populate every continent except Antarctica. Their habitats are varied, and their long host-plant list includes composites, legumes, borages, and mallows. Painted Ladies are so adaptable that they will eat even an artificial diet, enabling their caterpillars to live in thousands of homes and classrooms, where they can be raised from kits without the use of a single plant.

Children may discover the miracle of metamorphosis by observing container-raised Painted Ladies, but they miss the miraculous relationship between host plant and butterfly. This association has long been considered

Painted Lady on Common White Snakeroot

so important that another common name for Painted Lady is Thistle Butterfly. Within their broad host-plant palette, thistles are definitely favorites, and female Painted Ladies place single, barrel-shaped eggs within the down of fresh young leaves. Tiny caterpillars initially live below a thick layer of plant hairs, where they nibble holes into leaf surfaces and place themselves within the newly created windowpane. As larvae grow, they enlarge their territories and construct nests by loosely tying plant leaves together. Caterpillars come in several color forms and are as spiny as their thistle hosts (although their points are not nearly as painful). Their combined prickliness, along with the accumulation of frass that adheres to tacky thistle down, presents a formidable and unappetizing appearance to would-be predators. Final instar caterpillars often pupate within their messy nests.

Caterpillar (black form) on a thistle

The Painted Lady's worldwide occurrence has also earned the name "Cosmopolitan," but ironically, each year the species must recolonize much of its range, including Alabama. Why? Painted Ladies are not cold tolerant, and in North America, their primary permanent residences are in Mexico and the southwestern deserts of the United States. When spring arrives, they seem to sprint across the continent, sometimes outdistancing their Monarch compatriots. By April, we have found them in the chilly mountains of northeast Alabama. Large eruptions of Painted Ladies seem to coincide with abundant spring rains in their desert homes, and they can be quite common throughout their range. But not every year is good for population expansion. In spite of thousands of schoolyard butterfly releases, observers in Alabama may be lucky to see a Thistle Butterfly, aka Cosmopolitan, aka Painted Lady, at all.

Above: Painted Lady caterpillar (brown form) eating a rose-mallow bud

Opposite: Painted Lady on a blazing-star

Red Admiral *Vanessa atalanta*

According to legend, Red Admirals were named for their resemblance to eighteenth-century British naval uniforms. In addition to impersonating an officer, Red Admirals' velvety black-brown wings and crisp orange stripes create classic warning or aposematic color combinations. It may be a case of false advertising, for there is no evidence that these butterflies are unpalatable or poisonous.

Red Admirals appear pert and alert, often perching on open ground to display their distinctive colors or to sip minerals. Adults seek energy from sap and decomposing matter, but are also avid nectarers, visiting flowers such as milkweeds and asters. Caterpillar food is comprised primarily of nettles and false nettles, weedy plants that flourish in damp soil along swamp edges and stream banks as well as suburban yards. Cylindrical, bright blue-green eggs are laid singly on leaf tips. Caterpillars construct haphazard leaf nests

Red Admiral on a goldenrod

by silking several leaves together or by folding a single leaf to form a boxy enclosure. A look within these structures reveals not only the bristly larvae, but also an assortment of webbing, detritus, and frass—a messy room, but at least its occupant is invisible to searching predators. Caterpillars literally eat themselves out of house and home, and must construct several nests before pupating. In addition to hiding from predators, larvae also bristle with dangerous-looking barbed spines. Prickly but harmless, the effect is intensified if Stinging Nettle happens to be the chosen host. Gray-brown chrysalides are seldom seen, not only because they are well camouflaged, but also because they are often hidden within the caterpillars' final leaf shelter.

Each spring Red Admirals must recolonize much of their extensive North American range because of their intolerance of freezing temperatures. Fortunately, Alabama's climate allows these jaunty nymphalids to maintain resident populations throughout the year.

Caterpillar's leaf shelter in False Nettle

Red Admiral chrysalid

Red Admiral caterpillar after eating previous leaf shelter

Red Admiral on Sweet-Scented Joe-Pye-Weed

Mourning Cloak *Nymphalis antiopa*

Mourning Cloaks often surprise us by making an appearance on warm winter days, their elegant, glowing wings brightening dreary landscapes. One of Alabama's longest-lived butterfly species, adults spend wintry months in hiding spots, sheltered from the elements. Special chemicals in their blood called glycerols function like antifreeze, enabling them to withstand freezing weather. Not true hibernators, they stir whenever temperatures rise, shiver to help raise their own body temperatures, and search for nonfloral energy sources that may even include sap from sapsucker-drilled tree trunks. Worn survivors live well into spring, resume a normal lifestyle, and produce the next long-lived generation.

Mourning Cloaks use a variety of trees as larval hosts. It is one of at least five butterfly species that oviposits on hackberries. Other hosts, such as willows and cottonwoods, flourish in wetlands, but also extend into drier habitats, so Mourning Cloaks can be expected almost anywhere. Regardless of plant

Basking Mourning Cloak

selection, gravid females lay their eggs in large clusters that often encircle twigs. Young caterpillars are extremely gregarious, thrashing and twitching their bristly bodies in synchrony or dropping en masse to the ground when threatened. Two rows of red spots, echoed by outlandishly red legs, send a message of warning to would-be predators. The brood may disband in later stages, but sometimes final instar caterpillars line up on a branch, one next to the other, to form a row of chrysalides.

Although dozens of caterpillars may be found on one tree, multiple adults are rarely encountered—except in spring. Then, like many butterfly species, they engage in a mate location behavior called "hilltopping." Heading for the highest geographical point, they look for receptive members of the opposite sex. Once mated, females quickly retreat, but males often remain for days, aggressively defending prime territories. Mourning Cloaks are strong fliers and wanderers by nature. They seldom stick close to home—except in winter, when they patiently wait for a break in the weather.

Chrysalid suspended
from a willow branch

Above: Mourning Cloak on a lichen-covered log

Left: Mourning Cloak caterpillars with immature willow seed capsules

Question Mark *Polygonia interrogationis*

Question Marks look a lot like Comma Anglewings, but a single dot trans-forms their punctuation mark from a comma to a question mark—or is it a semicolon? In Gosse's day, field marks took a back seat to color, and Question Marks were known as Violet-Tips, another descriptive name because their wings are edged with lavender. Their heavily scalloped, uneven wing shape places them in a group of butterflies descriptively called anglewings (or polygonias, which means "many angled"). In Alabama, Question Marks are the largest of the bunch.

While their wings are always angled and their signature question mark is constant, the Question Marks' violet tipping is variable. They are seasonally variable (or dimorphic) and produce distinct forms with differing amounts of purple. Fall-spring butterflies possess longer tails and orange upper surfaces that are heavily outlined with lavender. Summer-generation hindwings are short tailed and almost black, their violet edging reduced to a thin line. All forms display cryptically and variably colored under surfaces, which com-bined with their jagged shapes make them excellent tree-bark mimics. To the bafflement of predators (and butterfly watchers), these butterflies can disappear by merely landing and closing their wings.

Question Mark caterpillars are numbered in the long list of hackberry-eating butterfly larvae, although they frequently utilize other Elm family members as well. Winged Elm is a favorite and on occasion, Question Marks share a taste for nettles with their Comma Anglewings cousins. Female Question Marks select tender leaves, often at eye level, and painstakingly stack sev-eral green, vertically ribbed eggs on leaf surfaces. Pillars of three or four are common, but we have observed as many as seven precariously balanced eggs. Caterpillars sometimes share leaves with their siblings, and since Ques-tion Marks are not tightly brooded, larvae of varying ages may feed in close proximity on the same branch. However, they typically feed in solitude. Stiff-

Opposite: Question Mark (winter form) on Winged Elm

Left: Question Mark perched on Winged Elm

Below: Question Marks (summer form) on a cypress knee

Opposite: Question Mark egg chain on a hackberry leaf

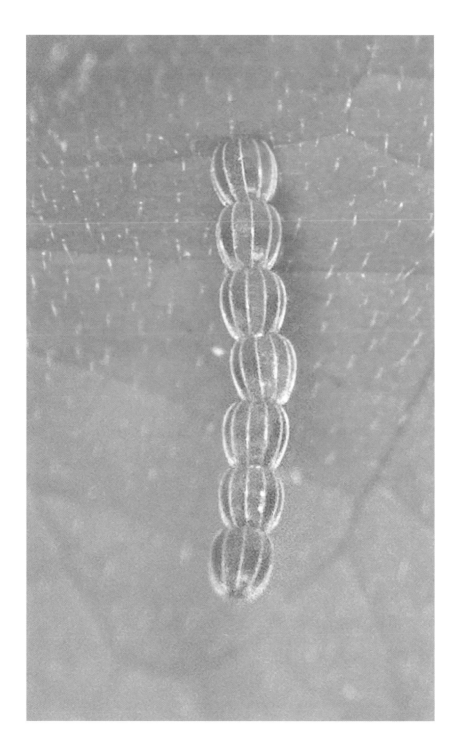

leaved host trees are not conducive to shelter building, so caterpillars depend on their fierce, heavily barbed appearance for protection against predation.

Because of their host-plant preferences, Question Marks often live near streams that flow along the edges of deciduous woods. They are regular visitors to puddles and creek banks, where they gather in numbers. Infrequent nectarers, they rely primarily on nonfloral food sources and sip juices from overly ripe fruit, animal dung, and oozing trees. Males are notoriously territorial and dart out to investigate almost any intruder. They return to the same reliable perch but may first stop to sample perspiration-damp skin.

Overwintering adult Question Marks fly on warm days and are often seen early in spring. A flash of orange wings along a woodland trail can leave observers wishing for a hindwing view in order to answer the age-old question, "Was it a Question Mark or a Comma?"

Question Mark
chrysalid suspended
from Winged Elm

Final instar Question Mark caterpillar on Winged Elm

Comma Anglewing *Polygonia comma*

Comma Anglewings seem to come out of nowhere on the earliest days of spring. Erupting from a sunny patch or a nearby tree trunk, they startle with an erratic flash of orange and then quickly disappear with the close of a wing. Since they often return to their original perches, they may surprise hikers both coming and going.

Comma Anglewings are slightly smaller than look-alike Question Marks, but the size difference is difficult to discern in the field. Their silver hindwing marking is a more dependable indicator—it lacks a dot and so resembles a comma . . . or a fishhook . . . or the letter "C." Comma wings are even more "angled" or jagged than Questions Marks and typically lack violet edging.

Comma Anglewing nectaring on Sweet-Scented Joe-Pye-Weed

They share the anglewing trait of feeding at sap flows, fruit, and carrion, but will also avidly nectar when these nonfloral food sources are in short supply.

In Alabama, Comma Anglewings produce at least three generations and two different color forms. Late-fall butterflies, whose upper surface (dorsal) hindwings are orange, overwinter and become active again in spring. Summer generations display dark, almost black, dorsal hindwings. Females are slightly larger than males, but are otherwise virtually identical in appearance.

Comma caterpillars are often found on nettles and false nettles, although hackberries are chosen occasionally. They emerge from eggs that are placed separately or stacked in small columns. Solitary eaters, first instar larvae chew tiny holes in host leaves. Older caterpillars eat all but the leaf vein, and

Comma
Anglewing
sipping from a
cypress knee

often fold under leaf edges to form loose shelters. Comma caterpillars are wickedly spiny, and each spine is also covered with barbs. Even their rounded heads are spiked, but none of these fierce weapons inflicts injury to humans.

Chrysalides resemble wilted brown leaves and are studded with silver or gold spikes. Their metallic ornamentation is the source of an interesting superstition as well as another longtime common name, Hop Merchant. In hop-growing states, Comma Anglewings regularly use these beer-flavoring herbs as caterpillar hosts. Their chrysalides often dangle from twining hop vines, so the gold or silver studded pupae are common sights to growers. According to legend, if the pupal spikes are golden, the price of hops will rise, but if they shine silver, prices will plummet.

Hops are rarely grown in Alabama, so Common Anglewings are not dependable price predictors. But after a cold winter, their renewed flights are reliable forecasts of spring.

Comma Anglewing (summer form) on Winged Elm

Comma Anglewing (winter form) on Sweet-Scented Joe-Pye-Weed

Comma Anglewing caterpillar on False Nettle

Common Buckeye *Junonia coenia*

In Alabama, Common Buckeyes are easy to identify. Beautiful and stunningly marked, a rainbow of colors ornaments a warm-brown background. Nothing else looks quite like them. Yet, despite their familiarity, Common Buckeyes are so highly variable in appearance that no two look exactly alike. Seasonal variations account for many of the differences. Wing colors are brightest late in the year, and fall generations sport rosy-red hindwings. Spring and summer forms are plainer and more uniformly tan. All buckeyes sport large, showy eyespots that dot opened wings, perhaps making them look like goggle-eyed monsters to potential predators.

Buckeye caterpillars draw on chemical as well as visual defense mechanisms. Host plants are typically members of the Figwort and Acanthus families and contain bitter iridoid glycosides, compounds produced by plants to

Common Buckeye on a thoroughwort

Common Buck-
eyes exhibit a
variety of color
forms as they
visit goldentops,
vervains, and
snakeroots

discourage herbivory. Larval buckeyes are not at all discouraged and sequester toxins as they eat. Flaunting their unpleasant taste with aposematic coloration, spiny caterpillars are easy to spot as they cling to slender host-plant
stems, unconcerned about their apparent vulnerability. Chrysalides resemble
shriveled dry leaves and appear to be bits of detritus as they dangle amid a
cloud of green foliage.

Common Buckeyes are habitat generalists, requiring little more than open,
sunny areas, and intermittent patches of bare ground for males to perch and
establish territories. Warm weather is another requirement, because buckeyes cannot withstand freezing temperatures in any stage of their life cycle.
In Alabama, they become especially common in the fall, when southward migrants boost our resident population of these rainbow-colored butterflies.

Above: Territorial male Common Buckeye on lichen and moss

Opposite: Common Buckeye caterpillar and chrysalid on a false foxglove

Baltimore Checkerspot *Euphydryas phaeton*

Baltimore Checkerspots and Baltimore Orioles were both named for the heraldic orange and black colors of Lord Baltimore, the seventeenth-century colonizer of Maryland. Three hundred years later, the bird has become known as the Northern Oriole, but the strikingly hued butterfly still retains its longtime moniker and exists in scattered colonies across the eastern United States.

The brilliant colors that we find so beautiful in Baltimore Checkerspots are alarming to many predators. These butterflies are unpalatable to birds, and the distinctively colored checkers serve as a warning signal. Like many "protected" butterflies, Baltimore Checkerspots can afford to be slow, deliberate fliers—at least when it comes to avoiding natural predators. They frequently puddle on roadsides and are so sedentary that passing cars run over them.

Baltimore Checkerspot on Butterfly Milkweed

The source of the Baltimore's toxicity originates with its host plants. Early in life, Baltimore Checkerspots are very host specific and select plants within the Figwort family, known for its iridoid compounds. For many years, turtle-heads (wetland figworts) were thought to be the only larval hosts, but Baltimore Checkerspot colonies were also discovered in dry, upland areas. There, butterflies oviposit on false foxgloves, figworts that inhabit rocky, oak wood-lands. In central Alabama, we have discovered caterpillars eating Smooth Yellow False Foxglove, even when large colonies of turtlehead were in close proximity.

Whether choosing upland or lowland figworts, Baltimore females de-posit clusters of several hundred tiny eggs on the undersides of host leaves.

Above: Caterpillar nest constructed in Smooth Yellow False Foxglove

Left: Overwintering caterpillars in leaf litter

Newly hatched larvae migrate to the tops of plants where they spin webs and feed communally. They gradually increase the size of the web to include more and more plant material, wandering outside their nest at times but always returning to its safety. In late summer, the larvae stop feeding and add substantially to their web. The longtime assumption was that they spent the winter in this nest, but the structure actually functions as a pre-hibernation site. Most caterpillars move out of it in late fall and descend into the leaf litter at the base of the plants where they overwinter. Warmer temperatures and longer days trigger a return to activity and eating, but neither foxgloves nor turtleheads have sufficient spring foliage to support the voracious appetites of growing caterpillars. In an unusual adaptation, many larvae desert their earlier hosts to chow down on a wide variety of herbaceous plants including plantain and penstemon, which also contain iridoid compounds. Chrysalides display orange and black markings on a creamy-white background—another interpretation of Lord Baltimore's basic color scheme.

Baltimore Checkerspots are on the wing only a few weeks in early to mid summer. They would be easy to overlook except for their exceptional beauty. Fortunately, their harlequin colors and slow, deliberate flight make them striking standouts. Lord Baltimore would be proud.

Left: Baltimore Checkerspot chrysalid with shed cuticle

Opposite: Baltimore Checkerspot on White Milkweed

Silvery Checkerspot on a sunflower

Silvery Checkerspot *Chlosyne nycteis*

At first glance, Silvery Checkerspots look a lot like crescents. However, a second look reveals that they are larger, higher-flying butterflies, and an even closer examination discloses their telltale lustrous hindwing checkers. Sometimes called Streamside Checkerspots, they form colonies in moist habitats where favorite host plants are common.

Composites such as sunflowers and rosinweeds are preferred larval food. Giant Ragweed is also eaten with gusto, striking a blow for hay fever sufferers everywhere. Many of these plant species grow side by side, and gravid females may utilize all of them as egg-laying sites. Emerging from large clusters of eggs stacked underneath leaves, multitudes of tiny caterpillars eat together during early instars. They lay down sticky silken thread paths to help the group stay together as it moves from one location to the next, and occupied sites are messy and obvious. The dark, bristly larvae become more solitary as they mature and often rest in plain sight on tops of host leaves. If a predator decides to risk an encounter with their fierce-looking spines, it must be quick, for these caterpillars curl and drop to the ground at the slightest hint of disturbance.

Habitat and host plants are plentiful throughout Alabama, and Silvery Checkerspot colonies are spread across the state, but they are not common. For unknown reasons, these butterflies have almost disappeared from the northeastern United States. Alabama's populations are poorly documented so no one knows if they are suffering the same fate. Careful monitoring is needed to assess the status of this colonial, ragweed-eating species.

Above: Silvery Checkerspot
caterpillars on a sunflower

Left: Silvery Checkerspot
chrysalid

Silvery Checkerspot on Ox-Eye Daisy

Gorgone Checkerspot *Chlosyne gorgone*

It's hard to keep track of Gorgone Checkerspots. Lucky butterfliers who have been fortunate enough to find them in the southeastern United States often discover that when they return the following year, Gorgones are nowhere to be seen. In Alabama, records from the 1950s indicated that these checkerspots were found in Calhoun and Cleburne counties. Currently, the records and subsequent populations of the butterflies are missing.

The species in question is a medium-sized checkerspot, somewhat larger than a Pearl Crescent but smaller than a Silvery Checkerspot. Although the Gorgone Checkerspot can be confused with similar species, highly patterned, zigzagged hindwing markings set it apart. Much more common in the Midwest than the Southeast, its populations probably moved eastward long ago, and today they exist in scattered, isolated colonies. Various dry, sunny sites sustain them, and often include open woods, fields, and power cuts, but Gorgone Checkerspots are vagrants. Adapted to early succession landscapes, they strike while the habitat iron is hot and then quickly move on.

Gorgone Checkerspot on a tickseed

Theoretically, Alabama's particular Gorgones (belonging to the subspecies "carlotta") produce at least two, possibly three broods each year. Details are sketchy, but the first generation probably flies in late spring (late April/May) and the second follows in midsummer. A partial autumn brood may also occur. Throughout much of their range, Gorgone Checkerspots use various sunflowers and possibly other composites as their host plants. While there are no confirmed hosts in Alabama, many composites occur within potential Gorgone habitats.

Like most checkerspots, Gorgones lay their eggs in tight clusters on host-plant foliage, and young larvae are extremely gregarious, communal feeders. Bristly caterpillars spin trails of silk and drop from plants if threatened. Three different color forms occur: basic black, orange/black combinations, and solid orange. Partially grown larvae overwinter.

Two hundred years ago, the famed entomologist/illustrator John Abbot painted a depiction of Gorgone Checkerspots based on butterflies he observed in Burke County, Georgia. The species was not documented there again until almost two centuries later, when the skilled lepidopterist Ron Gatrelle happened upon a colony while changing a flat tire on a rural roadside. If Gorgone Checkerspots are rediscovered in Alabama, we hope that there will not be another two-hundred-year gap between sightings.

Caterpillars on a sunflower

Gorgone Checkerspot on a tickseed

Texan Crescent *Anthanassa texana seminole*

Texan Crescents are the *dark* crescents that inhabit our state. Pearls and Pha-ons are orange butterflies with dark markings. Texan Crescents reverse the pattern. Located mainly within the Coastal Plain, they are bottomland but-terflies, preferring damp areas, often near creeks, lakes, or rivers. Unlike their more sun-loving relatives, they choose shaded edges and dappled sunlight, although they also bask and imbibe moisture on sandy riverbanks.

Texan Crescents nectar at many small flowers, including fleabanes and beggarticks, but host plants are members of the Acanthus family. Predomi-nately a tropical family, acanthus plants typically produce opposite leaves, unusually lipped flowers, and tissues that brim with burning calcium oxalate crystals. Loose-Flower Water-Willow is a common host in Florida, but in Ala-bama, we have found that Branched Foldwing is the acanthus of choice along the Alabama River and its tributaries. This lovely plant bears narrow two-lipped, pinkish-purple blooms in late summer and fall and is also known by the unfortunate name of Wild Mudwort (a nod to its moisture-loving nature). Texan Crescents seldom stray from host-plant vicinity and lay egg masses

Texan Crescent on beggarticks

underneath leaves, often selecting young, shaded plants. Dark-headed caterpillars emerge en masse and live communally throughout early stages of development. Moving like a tidal wave across a leaf's surface, they strip it of its tender epidermis, leaving only the lacy infrastructure. They do not construct nests, but lay many trails of silk, which not only anchor them to the plant, but also serve as roadmaps for sibling travelers. If startled, caterpillars drop from their leaves and dangle by single threads until danger has passed.

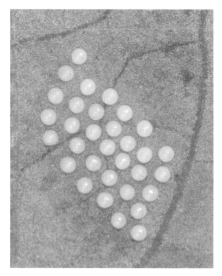

Left: Egg group on Branched Foldwing

Below: Early instar caterpillars on Branched Foldwing

As larvae mature, they tend to go their separate ways, but often still congregate in groups of two or three. Several broods occur each year, and partially grown caterpillars from the final brood overwinter. Chrysalides are plain brown structures that blend with stems, twigs, and withered leaves.

Texan Crescents range throughout the American Southwest, but Alabama's butterflies belong to the subspecies dubbed "seminole." These unique butterflies form scattered colonies throughout the southern coastal states. Although similar in many respects to their western cousins, they have larger orange wing patches and very different habitats. (Texas Texan Crescents live in dry gulches.) Some lepidopterists consider the differences significant enough to warrant separate species status, but currently the regional preferences of our Texan Crescents are only recognized by their designations as Seminoles—a Native American tribe that, like their namesake butterflies, once resided in Florida, Georgia, and Alabama.

Left: Texan Crescent chrysalid

Below: Final instar Texan Crescent caterpillar on Branched Foldwing

Texan Crescent on a sneezeweed

Phaon Crescent *Phyciodes phaon*

Phaon Crescents and Pearl Crescents often fly side by side in the Coastal Plain. Seemingly an identification nightmare, Phaons can be distinguished by the unique creamy band that bolts down both dorsal and ventral forewings. While both crescents love sunny habitats, Phaons usually stick to sites with very short vegetation that include roadsides, grazed pastures, low dunes, and even mowed lawns. They fly lower than their cousins, almost never rising more than six inches from the ground.

Phaon Crescents also separate themselves from Pearls by their host-plant choice. Pearls are aster eaters, but Phaons choose frogfruit (or phylas), a low-growing, mat-forming, moisture-seeking genus within the Verbena family. Formerly known as lippia, its club-shaped flowers are wreathed with tiny blossoms that are extremely attractive to many nectaring butterflies, including Phaon Crescents. Its unique floral shape earns frogfruit another common name: match heads. Like other Verbena family members, phylas contain bitter iridoid glycosides that possibly aid caterpillar and/or adult crescents in their own protection against predation. Phaon Crescents seldom stray far from frogfruit, and in Alabama, these butterflies should be sought wherever frogfruit is found.

Both male and female Phaons flutter only inches from the ground, remaining near their host-plant patches. Females occasionally stop to deposit clusters of creamy-white eggs on the undersides of phyla leaves. Like most crescent larvae, Phaons are communal and spend the first stages of their lives bunched with their siblings, eating tender leaf surfaces. Silken trails enable the group to keep in touch, and small nests surround foliage. Short stiff bristles cover the olive-brown larvae: from a distance, mature caterpillars appear to be nothing more than darkened, spent frogfruit flowers. Phaon Crescents produce several generations each year, and although they occur almost continuously on the coast, adults may enter reproductive diapause during winter.

Phaons are our southernmost crescents and rarely extend above the

Phaon Crescent on a daisy fleabane

Coastal Plain. Although small populations pop up at least as far north as the fish hatcheries in Perry County, they undoubtedly perish with the onset of freezing temperatures. Dauphin Island provides a more permanent home for these ground-hugging, brightly colored crescents.

Left: Phaon Crescent chrysalid

Below: Phaon Crescent on a daisy fleabane

Opposite: Phaon Crescent caterpillars on a frogfruit

Pearl Crescent *Phyciodes tharos*

Pearl Crescents flit across Alabama's fields, pastures, roadsides, open wood-lands, and suburban yards—anywhere asters flourish. Wet, dry, sunny, or in open shade, there is an aster for almost any habitat, and Pearl Crescents find homes there as well. They are our state's most common crescent and can be found throughout warm months. Although wing patterns may vary from season to season, Pearls are recognizable and familiar. Nectaring avidly on flowers that include Butterfly Milkweed, Black-Eyed-Susans, and (of course)

Pearl Crescent (male) on Black-Eyed-Susan

asters, they will contentedly share flower blossoms, slowly flapping as they drink.

Pearl Crescent caterpillars are aster-leaf eaters and choose from several species within this group of bewildering look-alikes. Not all asters are favored. New York and Heartleaf asters are repellant, while New England and White Panicle are delectable. Varying amounts of the chemical known as aromatic hydrocarbon germacrene D, which ovipositing females detect by tapping antennae on leaves, may be responsible for these preferences. Within chosen aster species, young, shaded plants are sought for egg laying.

Pearl Crescent (female) on Butterfly Milkweed

When they finally find an acceptable host, female Pearls cling to upper leaf surfaces while curling their abdomens underneath. They may remain virtually motionless for half an hour, carefully stacking minute white eggs, one by one, into highly organized clusters. Young caterpillars are gregarious, and stick closely together while eating and resting. Older larvae venture out on their own. Throughout spring and summer, one generation follows another, but as winter approaches, third instar caterpillars respond to shortened day lengths and find shelter in a curled leaf. They remain in diapause until spring, when eating resumes.

In Alabama, Pearl Crescents are so common that they are the yardsticks by which all other crescents are measured. When looking at a small orange and black butterfly, identifiers should ask, "Why is it *not* a Pearl Crescent?"

Final instar Pearl
Crescent caterpillar
on an aster

Left: Pearl Crescent chrysalid suspended from a dried aster

Below: Pearl Crescent (dorsal) on Black-Eyed-Susan

Goatweed Leafwing *Anaea andria*

Goatweed Leafwings have dead-leaf mimicry down to an art. Perched on tree trunks or fallen limbs, their subtly patterned underwings render them invisible. Should they fly, a sudden flash of their vividly orange upper surface is guaranteed to startle predators (and butterfly watchers). In the blink of an eye, the brightly colored butterfly disappears again by merely landing and closing its wings into camouflage position. Goatweed Leafwings even resemble *falling* leaves—if frightened, they drop to the ground and remain motionless.

"Leafwing" is a descriptive name choice, but "Goatweed" is also appropriate, for crotons (often called "goatweeds") are the leafwing butterflies' only larval hosts. Typically growing in dry, alkaline habitats, there are several native Alabama species, including the rare shrub, Alabama Croton, showiest of the bunch. Most are smaller and more herbaceous, but their leaves still fea-

Above: Goatweed Leafwing basking

Opposite: Goatweed Leafwing (summer form) on Hogwort

ture diagnostic silvery undersides. Hogwort (or Woolly Croton) is common in the Coastal Plain, and smoother leaved Prairie Tea extends the Goatweed Leafwing's range into fields, pastures, and prairie edges throughout much of the state. An ovipositing female places one large round egg on a croton leaf tip, sometimes depositing several on a single plant. Newly emerged larvae construct frass chains, curious structures devised by chewing away leaf material to expose only the midrib and then sticking frass pellets to its tip in order to lengthen it. Early instars rest at the very end, where they appear to be merely extensions of their chains. They leave the safety of this home base only to eat. Stout older larvae outgrow the fragile appendages and move to new leaves that they roll into tight tubes. Their sandpapery heads block the entrances as they rest within the shelters. Even when venturing out for nightly forages, the gray-green color and minute silvery dots of the leafwing caterpillars blend perfectly with croton foliage and stems. Chrysalides also mimic leaves, and the stocky structures often dangle from croton stems, where they resemble partially furled foliage, complete with leaf venation.

Adult Goatweed Leafwings spend the winter in hiding, surfacing only on warm days. The overwintering generation exhibits brighter color and a more exaggerated shape than summer broods. Males are more uniformly orange than females, which tend to be heavily marked. Since their short proboscises prevent them from gaining access to nectar, leafwings seldom visit flowers, preferring overripe fruit, carrion, or sap flows. Their falcate upperwings and short-tailed hindwings present an unmistakable silhouette, but they are most often seen as a fast-moving orange flash that is gone as quickly as it arrived.

Goatweed Leafwing caterpillar with frass chain

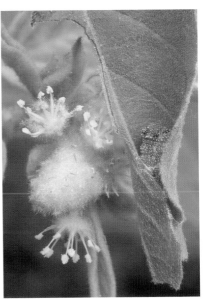

Clockwise from top:

Goatweed Leafwing caterpillar (head-on view) sitting on a frass chain

Caterpillar leaf shelter with resting Goatweed Leafwing caterpillar

Goatweed Leafwing (winter form)

Southern Pearly-Eye *Lethe portlandia*

Canebrakes are home to Southern Pearly-Eyes. Once covering vast expanses of lowland Alabama, according to the nineteenth century agronomist Edmund Ruffin, early settlers "could scarcely penetrate the close and general covering of cane."[15] The tough, rhizome-spreading plants were good fodder and, although able to survive the grazing of cattle, large cane populations succumbed to the conversion of fertile bottomlands to cotton fields. Today canebrakes are sparsely scattered along creeks and rivers. There, crepuscular Southern Pearly-Eyes often surprise visitors with ghost-like appearances as they flicker through dense growth of cane's reedy "culms" or stems.

Native Alabama canes are colonial, woody grasses that inhabit moist bottomlands within a forest understory. They are considered bamboos, and although they do not achieve oriental bamboo's extravagant heights, Giant Cane is sometimes called "tree grass" and may reach eighteen to twenty-five feet in optimal growing conditions. Switch Cane is typically shorter, but grows in the same habitats. Southern Pearly-Eye caterpillars are strictly cane feeders, and can be expected wherever it flourishes.

Female pearly-eyes deposit their opalescent round eggs on the undersides of cane leaves, sometimes placing them in small groups of two or three. Newly hatched larvae are as ghostly in appearance as their parents, but quickly turn either green or tan as they ingest foliage. Subtly striped caterpillars blend invisibly with the undersides of cane's parallel veined leaves, but their eating pattern is a give-away to the informed eye. Squared notches are eaten along the length of the blades and, when viewed from above, horned heads may sometimes be seen carefully chewing their way from top to bottom. Chrysalides are difficult to locate among an ocean of cane but are well worth the search, for the translucent green pendants are exquisitely beautiful. They are often suspended from their host cane's sturdy culms.

Southern Pearly-Eyes are quintessential examples of their group. Males perch head-down on tree trunks to await females, and adult energy sources

Opposite: Southern Pearly-Eye perched on Giant Cane

Left: Brown Southern Pearly-Eye caterpillar on Giant Cane

Below left: Southern Pearly-Eye chrysalid dangling from Giant Cane

Below right: Freshly emerged Southern Pearly-Eye

typically consist of decaying materials, sap, and other non-nectar nutrition. They are most active on cloudy days and at dusk, sometimes flying well after nightfall. Southern Pearly-Eyes often share their caney homes with Creole Pearly-Eyes, a similar sister species, but Southerns are generally more common and more frequently encountered. And, while pearly-eye wing patterns are very confusing, the Southern Pearly-Eyes' orange antennal clubs are a give-away to their unique identity.

Southern Pearly-Eye perched head down

Northern Pearly-Eye *Lethe anthedon*

Few butterflies haunt shady woodlands, but Northern Pearly-Eyes have found their niche there. Their opalescent forms seem to flicker through the understory, but disappear as soon as they land on bark or leaf litter. Like many of their satyr kin, they avoid strong sunlight and are most active on cloudy days and even at dusk. They are perfectly at home perched on tree trunks or sipping sap in shade so deep that few nectar-rich flowers exist.

Unlike other pearly-eyes whose caterpillars choose canes, Northern Pearly-Eyes eat grasses that have also adapted to dimly lit habitats. Females place a single egg or small groups of two or three ova underneath a chosen blade. Emergent tiny white larvae quickly turn green as they eat host grasses, chewing notches in typical satyr fashion. These caterpillars rely on crypticity and camouflage for protection. Their slow-moving, blade-like bodies appear flattened into the grass itself. Both tapered ends are also forked, possibly confusing predators as to the location of the all-important head. Late-season third or fourth instar caterpillars settle on a leaf's edge and spend winter months in diapause. Feeding resumes when new shoots emerge the following spring. Grass stems also make good pupation sites, where jade green chrysalides dangle like leafy earrings.

The woodland host plants most often selected by Northern Pearly-Eyes include River-Oats, White Cutgrass, and Eastern Bottlebrush Grass. All are shade-tolerant monocots that have adapted to low-light environments by developing broad leaf blades, which maximize sun exposure. Within the past century, another grass with the same features invaded the eastern woodlands. In 1919, Japanese Stilt Grass arrived in the United States as packing material in crates shipped from Asia. Today, it blankets woodlands with soft, harmless-looking foliage and displaces native species that are not able to compete with it. Currently, the impact of Japanese Stilt Grass on native communities is unknown. Closely resembling White Cutgrass, female pearly-eyes have found it acceptable for ovipositing, and caterpillars readily eat it. Time will tell whether the invasive stilt grass is friend or foe to Northern Pearly-Eyes and other woodland butterflies.

Northern Pearly-Eye on River-Oats

Northern Pearly-Eye caterpillar on partially eaten River-Oats

Left: Northern Pearly-Eye chrysalid suspended from River-Oats

Below: Perching Northern Pearly-Eye

Creole Pearly-Eye *Lethe creola*

Creole Pearly-Eyes are known for their knuckles: distinct forewing markings shaped like a closed fist. These ripply patterns distinguish them from look-alike Southern Pearly-Eyes, and this distinction is important, for Creole and Southern pearly-eyes are similar in almost every other way. Their physical resemblance is remarkable, but they also fly in the same habitats within the same time frames and presumably use the same host plants. Yet, for reasons we can only guess, Creoles are encountered with much less frequency than Southerns and are considered uncommon within their southeastern range.

Perhaps they were more prevalent before the demise of Alabama's vast canebrakes. Already on the way out when Philip Henry Gosse was writing his *Letters from Alabama,* he related that "the steep banks of many of the winding creeks and branches are densely clothed for considerable portions of their darkling course with tall canes," although "many of them have been cut down, and the depredations of cattle . . . prevent its attaining anything like the height and size which formerly characterized it."[16] Too bad, because dense canebrakes are exactly the sort of habitat where Creole Pearly-Eyes flourish. Basically shade-loving, crepuscular butterflies, they hide within thick undergrowth, often perching head down on tree trunks. Adults generally sip from sap flows, carrion, or damp earth, but their caterpillars are strictly cane eaters. In typical pearly-eye fashion, they chew distinctive notches from its blades. Slow-moving caterpillars often eat at night, which minimizes visibility to hungry eyes. Although they sport tiny red-tipped horns, their long thin shape and green or brown coloring provide perfect camouflage. Partially grown caterpillars overwinter within the cane patch.

Several theories have been offered to explain Creole Pearly-Eyes' comparative scarcity. One hypothesizes that they refuse Giant Cane and utilize only Switch Cane as caterpillar hosts. Another speculates that Creoles, particularly females, may merely be more reclusive than Southerns and so are less frequently encountered within thick undergrowth. A look at their range-wide population densities suggests that Creole Pearly-Eyes (despite the implica-

Perching Creole Pearly-Eye

tions of their name) are generally northeastern butterflies that have pushed the limits of their comfort zone by extending so far south. Whatever the reason, in Alabama, Creole Pearly-Eyes are seldom numerous and are usually outnumbered by their Southern Pearly-Eye counterparts.

Creole Pearly-Eye egg cluster on Giant Cane

Creole Pearly-Eye caterpillar on Giant Cane

Appalachian Brown *Lethe appalachia*

Appalachian Browns live among the sedgy edges of swamps, creek banks, and other wet spots. They are virtually always encountered under a shady, closed canopy and within sight of water. This particular niche has only recently been understood, because for many years, Appalachian Browns were considered part of a broader group of butterflies known as Eyed Browns. In 1947, the renowned University of Alabama biology professor Ralph L. Chermock recognized that within the larger group, a separate, more southern form existed. Full species status was awarded in the 1970s, and the name "Appalachian Brown" was coined.

The "Appalachian" adjective may be somewhat misleading, for we now know that these butterflies range well beyond the Appalachian Mountains, extending into central Florida and western Mississippi. "Brown" still hits the nail on the head, because only yellow-haloed eyespots adorn their otherwise mellow brown wings. Freshly emerged butterflies display traces of an icy blue sheen, but worn individuals are painfully plain and drab. Their nondescript color palette serves them well in their shady haunts. Even though they typically perch on green foliage, they are cryptic and camouflaged among surrounding tree trunks and ground litter.

Sedges, grasslike plants with three-sided stems, are clump-forming constituents of many wetland areas, and Appalachian Brown caterpillars feed on them. The larvae are exceedingly difficult to detect, closely resembling long slender sedge blades, especially when resting on a midrib. Their well-defined eating pattern is much more noticeable. Like most young satyrs, Appalachian Brown caterpillars chew distinctive, squared-off indentations into host leaves, creating deeper, more extensive notches as they grow. The cryptically colored crawlers look extremely slender because their heads and tails are exaggeratedly forked. Forward-pointing head horns are as long as the head is wide, and the tail is deeply cleft, causing both ends to look confusingly alike. Why this bit of deception? If a meal-seeking predator misses the all-important head and snaps at the tougher, less-sensitive hindquarters, caterpillars have a chance to escape by dropping to the relative safety of the

Appalachian Brown "just sitting"

ground. At least two generations of butterflies are produced each year and partially grown larvae overwinter. They turn as straw colored as a withered leaf blade and spend cold months tucked in just such a structure.

The Appalachian Browns' short proboscises prevent them from reaching the nectar of most flowers, and they typically take nutrients from sap, dung, carcasses, and mud. Not particularly social or colonial, they scatter within their shady, sedgy habitats. Typically, only a few are encountered at any one time. Despite their roaming tendencies, Appalachian Browns seem to spend a great deal of time just sitting. When disturbed, they fly far enough to find another suitable perch and "just sit" again.

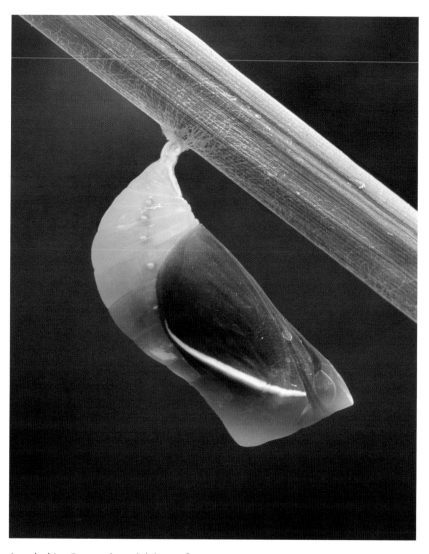

Appalachian Brown chrysalid (butterfly emergence is imminent)

Appalachian Brown caterpillar on sedge

Eastern Gemmed-Satyr *Cyllopsis gemma*

Eastern Gemmed-Satyrs are the only Alabama satyrs without discernable eyespots. Instead, their plain brown hindwings appear to be inlaid with tiny glittering baguettes. Set within a pearly oval, these decorations set gemmed-satyrs apart. The distinctive gems are faintly visible through their wings even when viewed from the top, although uppersides are seldom seen since Eastern Gemmed-Satyrs rarely bask with outstretched wings.

Among its satyr cousins, Gemmed is also unique because it exhibits two distinct seasonal forms in adult, larval, and pupal stages. Spring butterflies are dark and their markings are muted, perhaps masked by the darker scaling. Summer adults are lighter in color, and their markings are crisp and clear. Caterpillar differences are more dramatic. Those produced by the spring-flying generation are grass green, but their descendants are tan in color, enabling them to more effectively blend with maturing, straw-colored foliage. First-generation caterpillars typically produce green chrysalides, while the later generation produces light-brown pupae. Winter is generally spent in diapause as partially grown, tan-colored larvae.

Eastern Gemmed-Satyrs are often found in the company of Carolina Satyrs, although their plainer cousins usually outnumber them. Like Carolinas, they prefer moist, woodland habitats and their caterpillar host plants are shade-tolerant grasses like Slender Spikegrass. While Carolina Satyr caterpillars are stout bodied and round headed, Eastern Gemmed-Satyr larvae look long and lean, an illusion that is heightened because the length of their pointed horns exceeds the width of their head.

Eastern Gemmed-Satyrs skim the ground with their bouncy, bobbing flight. Males actively patrol for females and both sexes often stop to rest on leaf tips or open patches on the woodland floor. They also take sustenance from nutrients found in damp earth, sap, and various forms of decaying matter. These satyrs rarely nectar. We have found no records of this behavior in the literature and have witnessed it only once. In late May 2009, we were surprised to discover a single Eastern Gemmed-Satyr intently sipping nectar from American Wahoo flowers in Jackson County.

Above: Eastern Gemmed-Satyr
(summer form) resting on grass

Left: Chrysalid

When spring arrives, Eastern Gemmed-Satyrs are typically the first satyrs on the wing, and their tiny gems sparkle as they tilt their bodies toward the sun to more fully capture its rays. As John Henry Comstock and Anna Botsford Comstock commented in their 1907 book, *How to Know the Butterflies,* "The thrill of surprise one feels in discovering this exquisite decoration on such a dull insect is one of the experiences that renders the work of the butterfly lover never monotonous."[17]

Eastern Gemmed-Satyr caterpillar on partially eaten blade of grass

Eastern Gemmed-Satyr mated pair (spring forms)

Eastern Gemmed-Satyr nectaring on American Wahoo

Carolina Satyr *Hermeuptychia sosybius*

Carolina Satyrs are butterfly plain Janes and the smallest of Alabama's satyrs. Their muddy-brown hindwings are adorned only with darker-brown ripples and modest eyespots. When they bask, their fully extended wings open to reveal only more brown with no embellishment of any kind. As one butterflier put it, "Carolina Satyrs rarely perch with their wings open, and when they do, there isn't much to see."[18] Only swollen forewing veins that may function as auditory sensors break the expanse of dull, gray-brown scales. Some individuals are more heavily marked, and some display a purplish sheen when freshly emerged, but generally, Carolina Satyrs are monochromatic studies in basic brown.

Their color matches their habitat, for Carolina Satyrs are woodland butterflies. They are common throughout Alabama, especially in moist, forested areas. Constantly bobbing and weaving among grassy patches, Carolina Satyrs rarely rise more than a foot above the ground and appear to be searching for something they never find. Their seemingly purposeless movements are not as erratic as they look. Since these potentially tasty butterflies never fly in a straight line, they present confusing targets to predatory birds—difficult to capture and possibly not worth the effort. Male flight is anything but random: they constantly search for potential mates, tirelessly inspecting every nook and cranny of their grassy territories for unfound females. Carolina Satyrs often pause momentarily to rest from their wanderings, and both sexes settle in to dine at buffets of rotting fruit, animal droppings, fungi, and tree sap. Like many butterflies that reportedly never nectar at flowers, they do sometimes, especially in autumn.

During their seemingly random ramblings, female Carolina Satyrs occasionally stop to deposit single, round green eggs on or near low-growing grass blades. They accept native and introduced species, and readily use Bermuda Grass, St. Augustine Grass, and carpet grass, choosing plants that grow in dappled sunlight, near woodland edges. In an ironic twist of fate, this

Opposite: Carolina Satyr on bluestem grass

Above: Basking Carolina Satyr displaying very plain wings

Opposite: Carolina Satyr caterpillar on a bluestem grass

already common butterfly species has discovered and made host-plant use of highly invasive, forest-carpeting Japanese Stilt Grass, an exotic species that outcompetes and displaces many native plants on which other woodland butterflies depend.

Slow-moving, cryptically colored caterpillars are almost impossible to detect and often feed at night to lessen chances of discovery. Carolina caterpillar heads are bald compared to the horned heads of other satyr larvae, but like their relatives, their abdomens or "tails" are split into double prongs. Partially grown larvae overwinter in diapause and resume eating when spring brings a flush of new grass growth.

Mouse-brown Carolina Satyrs are not colorful attention grabbers, but these bobbing, bouncing little creatures are subtle beauties, and their trailside presence has provided companionship for many a hiker. In fact, when winter arrives, the woods seem empty in their absence.

Above: Carolina Satyr chrysalid on a bluestem grass blade

Opposite: Carolina Satyr nectaring on Woolly Elephant's-Foot

Georgia Satyr *Neonympha areolatus*

Georgia Satyrs are savanna butterflies—not Africa's rolling grass savannas, but the southern Coastal Plain's pine savannas. There, widely placed trees create open canopies where a diverse understory of low-growing plants receives sufficient sunlight to flourish. This community depends on periodic fires that are hot enough to keep shrubs from overgrowing and outcompeting diverse, ground-hugging vegetation, while leaving its pines undamaged. Within this ecosystem, Georgia Satyrs are primarily at home in wetland savannas, including pitcher plant seepage bogs.

Georgia Satyrs are small and drab, and only close observation reveals their lovely elongated hindwing eyespots, all encircled within a ring of orange. These satyrs bounce and bob among the low vegetation that blankets their favored habitat. Rarely flying more than a foot above the ground, they often choose to flutter through tall shrubs rather than over them. Males tirelessly patrol in search of mates, but females are reclusive, flying when flushed, then quickly dropping deep within undergrowth. Primary nutrition for both sexes comes from nonfloral sources including dung, sap, fungi, rotting fruit, and even pitcher plant secretions, but they also occasionally nectar at small flowers.

Sedges are common components of pine savanna understories, and they typically serve as Georgia Satyr host plants. Female satyrs cling to thin blades, curl their abdomens, and deposit pearly eggs, singly or in small clusters. Like other satyrs, Georgia Satyr caterpillars rely on camouflage as their primary defense against predation. Although their rounded heads are tipped with pert pink horns and their tails are split into two forks, larval shape and color closely match their host plant's slender green blades. Horizontal yellow-green stripes enhance crypticity, and when aligned with a leaf in typical resting position, caterpillars defy detection.

Longleaf pine savannas once dominated the southeastern landscape but are now one of the most-threatened ecosystems in the world. The Georgia Satyrs' dependence on savannas has only recently come to light. For more than a century, their unique characteristics were merged with that of a more widespread sister species now known as Helicta Satyr. Ron Gatrelle, founder

Georgia Satyr on a bluestem grass

Georgia Satyr sipping from Whitetop Pitcher Plant

Georgia Satyr caterpillar on a sedge

of The International Lepidoptera Survey (TILS), described both species and brought Georgia Satyr's separate identity into focus in 1999. Today this overlooked and misunderstood butterfly serves as a classic example and reminder of TILS's motto, "We cannot protect that which we do not know."

Above: Georgia Satyr chrysalid

Left: Georgia Satyr nectaring on a goldentop

Helicta Satyr *Neonympha helicta*

The classification and naming of butterfly species is an inexact science, and perhaps nothing illustrates this a well as the Helicta Satyrs' story. For two hundred years, small, bobbing, brown butterflies with orange hindwing halos were known as "areolatus" or Georgia Satyrs and considered at home in both upland and wetland habitats. Yet paintings by early-nineteenth-century naturalists clearly depict butterflies with two sets of similar but differing field marks. One, with rounder spots, was dubbed "helicta." Two centuries later, TILS founder Ron Gatrelle formally named and described Helicta Satyr as a separate species, based in part on specimens he collected near Foley, Alabama.

Helicta Satyrs are part of a confusing triad of closely related, visually similar butterflies in the genus *Neonympha.* Each species displays slight variations in wing markings, but habitat preferences are also important identity clues. The Georgia Satyrs' niche is low-lying, wet pine savannas. Mitchell's Satyrs choose beaver-impacted wetlands. Helicta Satyrs are the only high-ground dwellers and tolerate the driest habitats, including granite outcrops, upland pine savannas, and field edges. They typically fly higher and faster than either of their sister species as they bob over the tops of understory plants.

Sedges are preferred host plants, and female Helictas place their translucent eggs on thin blades, where they gleam like tiny pearls. Slow-moving, host-colored caterpillars disappear into a world of sedgy-green foliage. Within their chosen habitat, sedge plants are typically plentiful, but leaf content is high in difficult-to-digest silica and low in growth-enhancing nutrients, so caterpillar growth is slow. The first generation requires weeks to complete larval development, but the final brood takes even longer: it overwinters as half-grown caterpillars that resume their unhurried growth the following spring.

Species delineation of Helicta and Georgia Satyr remains murky and confusing. In the Coastal Plain, where both butterflies reside, many individuals display field marks of both species, making their identities too close to call.

Helicta Satyr perching near Eastern Prickly-Pear

Are they simply variants within two valid species, examples of possible hybridization between geographically close cousins, or evidence that a single, highly variable species actually exists? While lepidopterists scratch their heads in bewilderment, one thing is certain: whenever people try to neatly sort and categorize nature's vast diversity, the process is never simple.

Helicta Satyr chrysalid dangling from a sedge

Helicta Satyr caterpillar on a sedge

Mitchell's Satyr *Neonympha mitchellii*

On June 23, 2000, Dr. Jeffrey Glassberg, president of the North American Butterfly Association, and his wife, Jane Scott, casually focused their binoculars on a medium-sized brown butterfly resting on a Bibb County roadside. To their amazement, they saw Mitchell's Satyr—a critically imperiled, federally endangered butterfly whose nearest known population was more than five hundred miles away in North Carolina. Their chance discovery of a single butterfly sent conservation biologists scrambling to determine the extent and location of the Mitchell's Satyrs' population, its habitat requirements, and its life history. Intense searches for additional sites were pursued and over the next three years, several small, fragmented colonies were discovered within the Oakmulgee Ranger District of the Talladega National Forest.

The Mitchell's Satyrs' ecological niche in Alabama is only beginning to be understood, but it is clear that this butterfly is a habitat specialist. A wetland species, it bobs and weaves through vegetation that forms the interface between open, sunny marsh meadows and canopied swamp forests. Growing in only dappled sunlight, shrubs are numerous, but grasses, sedges, and rushes predominate. In Alabama, this unique habitat is most often created and maintained by long-term beaver activity.

Mitchell's Satyr resting
on Sensitive Fern

Mitchell's Satyrs avoid direct sunlight and are most active in late after-noons and on warm, overcast days. Males languidly patrol for females who spend most of their time resting beneath foliage, emerging when disturbed. Like other closely related satyrs, sedges are favored hosts, although in dense, tangled vegetation, eggs may be deposited on nearby plants, sending tiny larvae on a host-plant scavenger hunt. Caterpillars rely on camouflage for protection from the myriads of hungry insects, lizards, frogs, and birds that

Left: Mated pair

Below: Egg group on a grass

hunt in Alabama swamps. Cryptic coloration and blade-like shape virtually defy detection among dimly lit sedge leaves. Two distinct broods occur each year. The first flies in early summer, followed by a second, late-summer generation. Partially grown caterpillars overwinter.

The Mitchell's Satyrs' foothold in Alabama is precarious. Fire suppression and beaver eradication have threatened habitat creation and maintenance. Feral hogs are rampant in Bibb County and often trample and root in prime egg-laying sites. Even human observers are a source of danger as they walk through breeding areas, flattening potential host plants. In the midst of all these causes for worry, there is good news. Additional small colonies have been located since the initial Alabama surveys were completed and, in 2003, Mitchell's Satyrs were once again found in Mississippi. These recent discoveries strongly imply that this rare, secretive butterfly may be more common and widespread in the Southeast than originally thought.

Mitchell's Satyr
sipping from the
surface of a
Sensitive Fern

Mitchell's Satyr caterpillar on a sedge

Little Wood-Satyr *Megisto cymela*

Philip Henry Gosse sketched the Little Wood-Satyrs he saw in nineteenth-century Dallas County, Alabama. He commented that they, along with Carolina Satyrs, "chiefly affect the glades and lanes of the woods, being not very often seen in the clearing," and even when venturing into the garden, they behaved "as if shade were more congenial to their feelings than sunshine."[19] Today, Little Wood-Satyrs still bounce through grassy woodland edges, and although they may wander into open areas, they do not stray far from their forested habitats. Distinguished from Carolina Satyrs by their more prominent upper surface eyespots, as well as their dramatically eye-spotted underwings, Little Wood-Satyrs are also larger and display iridescent glints that their plainer cousins lack. They fly higher than the smaller satyrs, and often ascend into trees when alarmed.

Various grasses are host plants, and female Little Wood-Satyrs lay single, globe-shaped eggs on both living and dead blades. Caterpillars are short horned, forked tailed, and brown, but perhaps the most descriptive adjective for them is "slow"—everything about them is painstakingly slow. According to the nineteenth-century natural historian Samuel Scudder, they reposition themselves from blade to stem with movements that are "almost as difficult to see as the motion of the minute hand of a clock."[20] Development and growth seem interminable since each instar may last two weeks or longer. Late-season caterpillars extend their development by hibernating through winter months and do not resume their lethargic eating patterns until spring.

Much about Little Wood-Satyr's life remains shrouded in mystery. Exactly how many generations fly each year? Currently the answer is unknown. Some suggest that only one long, drawn out brood is produced. Others point to at least two population peaks that are composed of butterflies with slightly different appearances. One group separates Little Wood-Satyrs into types and refers to "Type One" and "Type Two" populations. Another suggests that these types actually represent two separate species and proposes a split.

An additional entity also figures into Little Wood-Satyr's confusing life

Perching Little Wood-Satyr

Above: Little Wood-Satyr displaying upper surface eyespots while nectaring on American Wahoo

Left: Little Wood-Satyr nectaring on American Wahoo

Opposite: Little Wood-Satyr caterpillar on bluestem grass

history. "Viola's" Wood-Satyrs (more spectacularly spotted, univoltine versions of the same basic butterfly) inhabit central Florida, and variously marked forms extend into the Panhandle as well as coastal Alabama. Lepidopterists have flip-flopped as to whether these more southern satyrs comprise their own species or are merely a subspecies of Little Wood-Satyr. As of this writing, those voting for subspecies status have won, and "Viola's" Wood-Satyrs are properly considered *Megisto cymela viola.* Clearly, when it comes to Little Wood-Satyrs, taxonomists have their hands full.

Little Wood-Satyr caterpillar (subspecies "Viola")

Little Wood-Satyr (subspecies "Viola") sipping from the surface of a dead leaf

Common Wood Nymph *Cercyonis pegala*

If prizes were awarded for best eyespots, Common Wood Nymphs would win hands down. Forewings, hindwings, upper surfaces, lower surfaces— no matter where you look, "eyes" look back. Common Wood Nymphs are geographically variable, but Alabama's particular subspecies flashes starling blue-pupilled eyes set in dramatic yellow patches. No wonder a once popular common name was Goggle-Eye.

Largest of the satyrs, Common Wood Nymphs inhabit tall grassy areas, wet meadows, upland fields, prairies, and open woodlands. They favor habitats with clump-forming native grasses such as bluestems and switch grasses. Although they will nectar at various wildflowers, they are typical satyrs and prefer to locate fermenting fruits, sap flows, or carrion.

Ironically, the Common Wood Nymph's life history reads more like a great-

Common Wood Nymph perched in leaf litter

er fritillary's than a typical satyr's. Like Great Spangled and Diana fritillaries, wood nymphs are univoltine and begin to fly in early summer. Males emerge as much as a week earlier than females. They are very visible as they actively patrol for partners, but females are more reclusive and tend to fly only when flushed. Males are short-lived and are typically gone before summer's end. Females live much longer and delay egg laying until late summer or early fall. They deposit round, yellowish ova on or near grass blades. When caterpillars hatch, they hide at the plant's base without eating. These first instar larvae hibernate through the winter, becoming active when grass begins to grow the following spring. Caterpillar development is slow, and the round-headed, subtly green-striped caterpillars take weeks to reach maturity. Chrysalides often hang from stems within the clumpy grass, and fresh butterflies finally emerge in early summer.

Common Wood Nymphs go to great lengths to evade potential predators.

Basking Common Wood Nymph

When alarmed, they quickly dart into grassy thickets or perch on bark, where their striated brown underwings allow them to disappear. If danger is close at hand, they feign death by falling to the ground, completely catatonic. But sometimes the tables are turned: sometimes potential predators are scared to death when they look up at a tree trunk only to discover a pair of disconcerting eyes glaring back at them.

Common Wood Nymph caterpillar on a blade of grass

Above: Common Wood Nymph concealed on bark

Left: Common Wood Nymph perched on a tree trunk

Focus on the Future

"Where are all the butterflies?" People often ask this question, and their fond reminiscences of childhood butterfly encounters usually follow. "Butterflies are still here," we answer. "Open your eyes and really look. Plant more flowers in your garden; add some host plants, and you will see butterflies." But nagging questions linger. Are butterflies really here in the numbers they were fifty years ago? Are they as widespread? Are there still places where the air "swarms" with butterflies as it did in Philip Henry Gosse's era? Do they "rise in clouds" in the same numbers as described by Dr. Ralph Chermock on a warm spring day in 1952? The answer is that no one knows.

Alabama ranks third among the fifty states in biodiversity, but its butterfly populations are understudied and poorly understood. Other states have made butterflies a higher priority. Connecticut, Massachusetts, and Vermont have a long history of lepidoptery and have recently completed butterfly atlas projects. North Carolina has an ongoing reporting program that culminates each year in the newest iteration of the "Approximation." A read-through of these materials enlightens us about the status of butterfly populations in these regions. We learn that while some species are stable, others are declining, and still others are imperiled. Some are even increasing in number. Conservation concerns are numerous, but habitat loss and fragmentation consistently and overwhelmingly top the list.

Habitat loss is an issue hauntingly familiar to Alabamians. It is echoed in the Alabama Wildlife Action Plan of our own Department of Conservation and Natural Resources (DCNR), which was put in to place in 2002. When drafting the plan, its developers reached a clear consensus: statewide, the primary threat to wildlife species is the historic and ongoing destruction and degradation of habitat.

Habitat is lost in many ways. Much results from development pressures associated with an increasing number of humans. From 1990 to 2000, Alabama experienced a 10.1 percent increase in population. From 2000 to 2025, the U.S. Census Bureau estimates that the the population will increase by 17 percent. An estimated 5.22 million people will live within the boundaries of this state, and urban and suburban footprints will expand to accommodate them.

Encroaching development is not the only threat to native habitats. Many naturally occurring forests have already been converted to intensively managed pulpwood productions. In these "pine plantations" the integrity and diversity of the natural community is lost, replaced by a prevailing monoculture. At least 5.5 million acres have been converted. Additionally, many areas that were historically dominated by Longleaf Pine have now transitioned to hardwood forests as a result of fire suppression. Once considered essential to woodland survival, preventing forest fires has had disastrous unintended consequences. Surviving forests now often have flammable, dense understories that burn too intensely for even fire-dependent longleafs.

Nonnative plant and animal species add their own set of imposing problems to Alabama's natural communities. Kudzu has become a familiar part of the Alabama landscape. Sometimes viewed humorously, it is no laughing matter—more than 250,000 acres are smothered with its tri-lobed foliage and deep-set tubers. Less familiar to many Alabamians but potentially even more dangerous is Cogon Grass, a fast-growing Asian weed that initially hitchhiked to Mobile as packing material. It is a hot-burning fire hazard, squeezes out native plants, ruins habitats, and is even more aggressive and harder to eradicate than Kudzu. Japanese Honeysuckle, Chinese Privet, Multiflora Rose, Chinese Tallow-Tree . . . the list of dangerous invasive aliens goes on. And it is not restricted to members of the plant kingdom. Feral hogs trample prime Mitchell's Satyr habitat, and introduced ladybird beetles, fire ants, and tachinid flies make meals of butterfly caterpillars. A Southeast Asian ambrosia beetle and the fungus it distributes threaten an entire genus of plants that are the sole hosts for the Palamedes and Spicebush Swallowtails.

What can be done to protect butterflies and other wildlife? Some steps are obvious: important natural habitats must be conserved and properly man-

Palamedes Swallowtail caterpillar on imperiled redbay

aged, using controlled burns when appropriate. Invasive, exotic species must be stopped in their tracks, and new intruders must be kept at bay. These priorities are important for all wildlife. But another problem must be addressed if we are to specifically and effectively conserve Alabama's butterflies. The initial Alabama Wildlife Action Plan did not include butterflies in the list of animals to be protected. So little was known about the current status of most species that accurate needs assessments were impossible. According to the plan's developers, "The lack of information on most invertebrate groups is a serious and significant gap in state and regional wildlife conservation which needs to be addressed."[1] We believe that citizen scientists have an important role to play in addressing this shortfall. By recording butterfly sightings and submitting this data to the state's Natural Heritage database (the depository for records of species that occur in Alabama), butterfly watchers, collectors, and other enthusiasts can significantly contribute to the conservation knowledge base. Locating and tracking rare species is important, but accurate data is also needed for common species so that their population trends can be tracked over time. With this information in hand, convincing arguments can be made about what species need protection, and wildlife conservation professionals can make informed decisions about when, where, and how to intervene.

To find out more about the Alabama Wildlife Action Plan and to support the inclusion of butterflies in its next revision, contact the Alabama Division of Wildlife and Freshwater Fisheries, Attn: Wildlife Diversity Coordinator, 64 N. Union Street, Montgomery, Alabama 36130.

For more information about how to report butterfly sightings, contact the Alabama Division of Wildlife and Freshwater Fisheries, State Lands Division, Natural Heritage Section, 64 N. Union Street, Montgomery, Alabama 36130, (334) 242-3484.

We cannot revisit and reconstruct the butterfly populations of the past, but we can study and quantify those of the present. Then, our hope is that in the future when people ask, "Where are all the butterflies?" Alabamians will know the answer.

Cloudless Sulphur immersed in American False Bindweed

Plant and Animal Associates

Animal and plant names are not uniform, and several credible lists are available for each. With few exceptions, we chose to follow the Butterflies of America interactive Web site in its selection of butterfly names. Plant nomenclature was chosen in an effort to follow that used in the upcoming revision of *Wildflowers of Alabama and Adjoining States*, an addition to the Gosse Nature Guide series.

Acanthus family (*Acanthaceae*)

Alabama Croton (*Croton alabamensis*)

Alder (*Alnus* spp.)

Alfalfa (*Medicago sativa*)

Ambrosia beetle (*Xyleborus glabratus*)

American Beech (*Fagus grandifolia*)

American False Bindweed (*Calystegia sepium*)

American Holly (*Ilex opaca*)

American Joint-Vetch (*Aeschynomene americana*)

American Mistletoe (*Phoradendron leucarpum*)

American Wahoo (*Euonymus atropurpureus*)

American Witch-Hazel (*Hamamelis virginiana*)

Appalachian-native Silvery Blue subspecies (*Glaucopsyche lygdamous lygdamous*)

Aster family (*Asteraceae*)

Aster (*Symphyotrichum* or *Eurybia* spp.) [*Aster* spp.]

Atlantic White-Cedar (*Chamaecyparis thyoides*)

Autumn-Olive (*Elaeagnus umbellata*)

Azure Blue Sage (*Salvia azurea*)

Baptisia (*Baptisia* spp.)

Batis family (*Bataceae*)

Beaked Hazelnut (*Corylus cornuta*)

Bear's-Foot or Yellow-Flower Leafcup (*Smallanthus uvedalius*)

Beaver (*Castor canadensis*)

Beggarticks (*Bidens pilosa*) [*Bidens alba*]

Bermuda Grass (*Cynadon dactylon*)

Blackberry (*Rubus* spp.)

Black Cherry (*Prunus serotina*)

Black-Eyed-Susan (*Rudbeckia hirta*)

Blazing-star (*Liatris* spp.)

Blueberry (*Vaccinium* spp.)

Blue Mistflower or Wild Ageratum (*Conoclinium coelestinum*)

Bluestem (*Andropogon* and *Schizachyrium* spp.)

Boogie-Woogie Aphid or Beech Blight Aphid (*Grylloprociphilus imbricato*)

Branched Foldwing *(Dicliptera brachiata)*

Brazilian Vervain *(Verbena brasiliensis)*

Buckwheat family *(Polygonaceae)*

Butterfly Milkweed *(Asclepias tuberosa)*

Cabbage *(Brassica oleracae)*

Cardinal-Flower *(Lobelia cardinalis)*

Carolina Redroot *(Lachnanthes caroliana)*

Carolina Vetch *(Vicia caroliniana)*

Carpet grass *(Axonopus* spp.)

Carrot family or Carrot/Parsley family *(Apiaceae)*

Chinese Mustard *(Brassica juncea)*

Chinese Privet *(Ligustrum sinense)*

Chinese Tallow-Tree or Popcorn-Tree *(Triadica sebifera)*

Citrus family *(Rutaceae)*

Climbing Hempvine *(Mikania scandens)*

Clover *(Melilotus* and *Trifolium* spp.)

Coastal Sea-Rocket *(Cakile lanceolata)*

Cogon Grass *(Imperata cylindrica)*

Common Black-Cohosh *(Actaea racemosa)*

Common Golden Alexanders *(Zizia aurea)*

Common Milkweed *(Asclepias syriaca)*

Common New Jersey-Tea *(Ceanothus americanus)*

Common Partridge-pea *(Chamaecrista fasciculata)*

Common Pawpaw *(Asimina triloba)*

Common Rue *(Ruta graveolens)*

Common White Snakeroot *(Ageratina altissima)*

Corn *(Zea mays)*

Cotton *(Gossypium* spp.)

Cottonwood *(Populus* spp.)

Cow-pea *(Vigna* spp.)

Cress *(Arabis* spp.)

Crimson Clover *(Trifolium incarnatum)*

Crotons *(Croton* spp.)

Crownbeard *(Verbesina* spp.)

Cudweed *(Gamochaeta* spp.)

Curly Dock *(Rumex crispus)*

Custard-Apple family *(Annonaceae)*

Cypress or Pond-Cypress *(Taxodium ascendens)*

Daisy fleabane *(Erigeron* spp.)

Dalea *(Dalea* spp.)

Dandelion or Common Dandelion *(Taraxacum officinale)*

Dill *(Anethum graveolens)*

Dock *(Rumex* spp.)

Dogwood *(Cornus* spp.)

Eastern Bottlebrush Grass *(Elymus hystrix)*

Eastern Prickly-Pear *(Opuntia humifusa)*

Eastern Purple-Coneflower *(Echinacea purpurea)*

Eastern Redbud *(Cercis canadensis)*

Eastern Red-Cedar *(Juniperus virginiana)*

Elm family *(Ulmaceae)*

False foxglove *(Agalinis* and *Aureolaria* spp.)

False Indigo or Tall Indigo-Bush *(Amorpha fruticosa)*

False Nettle *(Boehmeria cylindrica)*

False nettle *(Boehmeria* spp.)

Feral hog *(Sus scrofa)*

Figwort family *(Scrophulariaceae)*

Fire ant *(Solenopsis* spp.)

Flowering Dogwood *(Cornus florida)*

Flowering plum *(Prunus* spp.)

Fringed Bluestars *(Amsonia ciliata)*

Frogfruit *(Phyla* spp.)

Garden bean *(Phaseolus* spp.)

Garlic-Mustard *(Alliaria petiolata)*

Gattinger's Prairie-Clover *(Dalea gattingeri)*

Giant Cane *(Arundinaria gigantea)*

Giant Ragweed *(Ambrosia trifida)*

Glasswort *(Salicornia* spp.)

Goatweed *(Croton* spp.)

Goldenrod *(Solidago* spp.)

Goldentop *(Euthamia* spp.)

Groundsel *(Packera* spp.) *[Senecio* spp.]

Groundsel-Tree *(Baccharis halimifolia)*

Gulf Coast Swallow-Wort *(Cynanchum angustifolium)*

Hackberry *(Celtis* spp.)

Hairy Angelica *(Angelica venenosa)*

Hawthorn *(Crateagus* spp.)

Heartleaf Aster *(Symphyotrichum cordifolium)* [Aster cordifolius]

Heath *(Ericaceae)*

Heath family *(Ericaceae)*

Heliotrope *(Heliotropium* spp.)

Hibiscus *(Hibiscus* spp.)

Hickory *(Carya* spp.)

Hogwort or Woolly Croton *(Croton capitatus)*

Hops or Common Hops *(Humulus lupulus)*

Hoptree or Wafer-Ash *(Ptelea trifoliata)*

Horrid Thistle *(Cirsium horridulum)*

Horse-Sugar or Sweet-Leaf *(Symplocos tinctoria)*

Huckleberry *(Gaylussacia* spp.)

Introduced ladybird beetles *(Harmonia axyridis)*

Ironweed *(Vernonia* spp.)

Japanese Stilt Grass *(Microstegium vimineum)*

Joe-Pye-Weed or Trumpet-Weed *(Eutrochium* spp.)

Joint-vetch *(Aeschynomene* spp.)

Knotweed *(Polygonum* spp.)

Kudzu *(Pueraria montana)*

Lantana *(Lantana* spp.)

Laurel family *(Lauraceae)*

Legume *(Fabaceae)*

Lespedeza *(Lespedeza* spp.)

Live oak *(Quercus* spp.)

Live Oak *(Quercus virginiana)*

Loblolly Pine *(Pinus taeda)*

Longleaf Pine *(Pinus palustris)*

Loose-Flower Water-Willow *(Justicia ovata)*

Lupine *(Lupinus* spp.)

Mallow *(Malvaceae)*

Maryland Golden-Aster *(Chrysopsis mariana)*

Milkweed *(Asclepias* spp.)

Mint *(Mentha* spp.)

Mock bishopweed *(Ptilimnium* spp.)

Mountain-Laurel *(Kalmia latifolia)*

Mountain-mint *(Pycnanthemum* spp.)

Multiflora Rose *(Rosa multiflora)*

Mustard *(Brassicaceae)*

Native azalea *(Rhododendron* spp.)

Nettle (Urtica spp.)

New England Aster (Symphyotrichum novae-angliae)

New York Aster (Symphyotrichum novi-belgii)

"Northern" Oak Hairstreak (Satyrium favonius ontario)

"Northern" Silvery Blue (Glaucopsyche lygdamus couperi)

Northern Spicebush (Lindera benzoin)

Oak (Quercus spp.)

Oak Ridge Lupine or Blue Sandhill Lupine (Lupinus diffusus)

Ox-Eye Daisy (Leucanthemum vulgare)

Partridge-pea (Chamaecrista spp.)

Passion-flower (Passiflora spp.)

Pawpaw (Asimina spp.)

Pea family or Pea/Bean family (Fabaceae)

Pencil-flower (Stylosanthes spp.)

Phlox (Phlox spp.)

Pine (Pinus spp.)

Pipevine (Aristolochia spp.)

Pipevine or Woolly Dutchman's-Pipe (Aristolochia macrophylla)

Plantain-Leaf Pussytoes (Antennaria plantaginifolia)

Poke Milkweed (Asclepias exaltata)

Poorman's Pepperwort or Virginia Peppergrass (Lepidium virginicum)

Prairie-Tea (Croton monanthogynus)

Praying Mantis or Carolina Mantis (Stagmomantis carolina)

Privet (Ligustrum spp.)

Puff (Neptunia spp.)

Purple Crown-Vetch (Coronilla varia)

Purple Passion-Flower (Passiflora incarnata)

Purple Prairie-Clover (Dalea purpurea)

Purple-Top Vervain (Verbena bonariensis)

Pussytoes (Antennaria spp.)

Queen Anne's-Lace or Wild Carrot (Daucus carota)

Ragweed (Ambrosia spp.)

Rattlebox (Crotalaria spp.)

Redbay or Red Bay (Persea borbonia)

Redbay Ambrosia Beetle (Xyleborus glabratus)

Redbay (Persea spp.)

Redbay Psyllid (Trioza magnoliae)

Redbud (Cercis canadensis)

Red Clover (Trifolium pratense)

River-Oats (Chasmanthium latifolium)

Rose family (Rosaceae)

Rose-mallows (Hibiscus spp.)

Saltwort (Batis maritima)

Sassafras (Sassafras albidum)

Savannah Sunflower (Helianthus heterophyllus)

Scrub oaks (Quercus spp.)

Sedge (Carex spp.)

Sennae (Senna spp.)

Sensitive-brier (Schrankia spp.)

Sensitive Fern (Onoclea sensibilis)

Sheep Sorrel (Rumex acetosella)

Shoreline Sea-Purslane (Sesuvium portulacastrum)

Side-Beak Pencil-Flower (Stylosanthes biflora)

Slender Spikegrass (Chasmanthium laxum)

Small-Fruit Pawpaw *(Asimina parviflora)*

Smooth Yellow False Foxglove or Smooth Yellow Foxglove *(Aureolaria flava)*

Snakeroot *(Ageratina* spp.*)*

Sneezeweed *(Helenium* spp.*)*

Sourwood *(Oxydendrom arboreum)*

"Southern" Oak Hairstreak *(Satyrium favonius fixsenia)*

Southern Prickly-Ash or Hercules' Club *(Zanthaxylum clava-herculis)*

Southern Sundial Lupine *(Lupinus perennis)*

Sparkleberry *(Vaccinium arboreum)*

Spicebush *(Lindera* spp.*)*

St. Augustine Grass *(Stenotaphrum secundatum)*

Stiff Tickseed *(Coreopsis palmata)*

Stinging Nettle *(Urtica dioica)*

Strawberry *(Fragaria* spp.*)*

Sugarberry or Southern Hackberry *(Celtis laevigata)*

Sumac *(Rhus* spp.*)*

Sunflower *(Helianthus* spp.*)*

Swamp Dock *(Rumex verticillatus)*

Swamp Dogwood *(Cornus foemina)*

Swamp Milkweed *(Asclepias incarnata)*

Swamp Redbay or Swamp Bay *(Persea palustrus)*

Swamp Titi *(Cyrilla racemosa)*

Sweet-Bay Magnolia *(Magnolia virginiana)*

Sweet-Scented Joe-Pye-Weed *(Eutrochium purpureum)*

Switch Cane *(Arundinaria tecta)*

Switch grass or witch grass *(Panicum* spp.*)*

Tachinid fly *(Tachinidae* spp.*)*

Tall Thoroughwort *(Eupatorium altissimum)*

Thistle *(Cirsium* spp.*)*

Thoroughwort *(Eupatorium* spp.*)*

Tickseed *(Coreopsis* spp.*)*

Tick-trefoil *(Desmodium* spp.*)*

Toothwort *(Cardamine* spp.*)*

Trumpet-Creeper *(Campsis radicans)*

Trumpet-Weed or Hollow-Stem Joe-Pye-Weed *(Eutrochium fistulosus)*

Tulip-Poplar *(Liriodendron tulipifera)*

Turtlehead *(Chelone* spp.*)*

Vanilla-Leaf *(Carphephorus odoratissimus)*

Verbena family *(Verbenaceae)*

Vetch *(Vicia* spp.*)*

Violet *(Viola* spp.*)*

Virginia Goats'-Rue *(Tephrosia virginiana)*

Virginia Pine *(Pinus virginiana)*

Virginia-Snakeroot *(Aristolochia serpentaria)*

Virginia Sweetspire *(Itea virginica)*

Wax-myrtle *(Morella* spp.*)* [*Myrica* spp.]

White Crownbeard *(Verbesina virginica)*

White Cutgrass *(Leersia virginica)*

White Oak *(Quercus alba)*

White Panicled Aster *(Symphyotrichum laceolatum)*

White Prairie-Clover *(Dalea candida)*

Whitetop Pitcher-Plant *(Sarracenia leucophylla)*

Wild Bergamot *(Monarda fistulosa)*

Wild Blue Phlox or Eastern Blue Phlox *(Phlox divaricata)*

Wild Geranium *(Geranium maculatum)*

Wild indigo *(Baptisia* spp.*)*

Wild plum *(Prunus* spp.*)*

Willow *(Salix* spp.*)*

Winged Elm *(Ulmus alata)*

Wingstem *(Verbesina* spp.*)*

Wood ant *(Formica* spp.*)*

Woodland Stonecrop *(Sedum ternatum)*

Woolly Elephant's-Foot *(Elephantopus tomentosa)*

Woolly Ragwort *(Packera tomentosa) [Senecio tomentosus]*

Yellow False Garlic *(Nothoscordum bivalve)*

Yellow Passion-Flower *(Passiflora lutea)*

Yellow Sweet-Clover or White Sweet-Clover *(Melilotus officinalis)*

Butterflies of Alabama: An Annotated Checklist

Range Maps are based on information derived from the Butterflies and Moths of North America Web site, a searchable database of verified butterfly and moth records in the United States and Mexico, as well as our own observations and personal communications. The butterflies listed here appear in the same order as in the text. See page 448 for a key to Alabama's counties.

Swallowtails

Pipevine Swallowtail *(Battus philenor)*

Flight Time: Spring through fall.

Adult Energy Sources: A wide variety of flowers, including long-tubed blossoms like native azaleas.

Larval Hosts: Plants in the Birthwort family (Aristolochiaceae) including pipevines *(Aristolochia* spp.) and Virginia-Snakeroot *(A. serpentaria).*

Preferred Habitats: Usually in or near deciduous woodlands. Found in open habitats including gardens.

ID Tips: Dorsally, black with blue iridescence but no red or orange.

Note: Flutters constantly while nectaring.

Zebra Swallowtail *(Eurytides marcellus)*

Flight Time: Spring through fall.

Adult Energy Sources: A wide variety of flowers, although short proboscis length eliminates many long-tubed swallowtail favorites.

Larval Hosts: Shrubs in the Custard-Apple family (Annonaceae) including Common Pawpaw *(Asimina triloba)* and Small-Fruit Pawpaw *(A. parviflora)*.

Preferred Habitats: Hardwood forests as well as bottomlands. Tolerates development poorly.

ID Tips: Black and white stripes distinguish it from all other butterflies in the region.

Black Swallowtail *(Papilio polyxenes)*

Flight Time: Late spring through fall.

Adult Energy Sources: A wide variety of flowers, including long-tubed blossoms like native azaleas.

Larval Hosts: Herbs in the Carrot/Parsley family (Apiaceae) including native, naturalized, and cultivated family members.

Preferred Habitats: Various open places including fields and gardens.

ID Tips: Dark body with creamy-yellow dots. On both ventral and dorsal surfaces, look for a red spot with a black center at corner of hindwing.

Giant Swallowtail *(Papilio cresphontes)*

Flight Time: Spring through fall.

Adult Energy Sources: A wide variety of flowers, including long-tubed blossoms like native azaleas.

Larval Hosts: Citrus/Rue family (Rutaceae) members including Hoptree *(Ptelea trifoliate)* and Southern Prickly-Ash *(Zanthaxylum clava-herculis)*. Will utilize Common Rue *(Ruta graveolens)* in gardens.

Preferred Habitats: Ranges widely across open areas.

ID Tips: Predominately brown on dorsal surface, predominantly creamy yellow on ventral surface.

Appalachian Tiger Swallowtail *(Papilio appalachiensis)*

Flight Time: Spring.

Adult Energy Sources: Nectar sources are not well documented in Alabama. Blackberry blossoms are confirmed.

Larval Hosts: Undocumented.

ID Tips: Difficult to distinguish from Eastern Tiger Swallowtail. "Appy" hindwings are more elongated and triangular. About 20 percent larger than first-generation Eastern Tigers.

Note: A newly described species. Much, including range, is unknown.

Eastern Tiger Swallowtail *(Papilio glaucus)*

Flight Time: Early spring through fall.

Adult Energy Sources: A wide variety of flowers, including long-tubed blossoms like native azaleas.

Larval Hosts: In Alabama, Black Cherry *(Prunus serotina)* in the Rose family (Rosaceae) and Sweet-Bay Magnolia *(Magnolia virginiana)* and Tulip-Poplar *(Liriodendron tulipifera)* in the Magnolia family (Magnoliaceae) are confirmed. Hosts from other families may also be used.

Preferred Habitats: Almost anywhere with deciduous trees, especially in edges and openings.

ID Tips: Background color may be yellow or black but black stripes are always visible, especially on the ventral surface.

Spicebush Swallowtail *(Papilio troilus)*

Flight Time: Spring through fall.

Adult Energy Sources: A wide variety of flowers, including long-tubed blossoms like native azaleas.

Larval Hosts: Trees and shrubs in the Laurel family (Lauraceae), especially Sassafras *(Sassafras albidum)* and Northern Spicebush *(Lindera benzoin)*.

Preferred Habitats: Generally along deciduous woodland borders and bottomlands.

ID Tips: Blue scaling splits inner row of orange spots on ventral hindwing.

Note: Flies more slowly than other swallowtails.

Palamedes Swallowtail *(Papilio pala-medes)*

Flight Time: Spring through fall.

Adult Energy Sources: A wide variety of flowers, including long-tubed blossoms like native azaleas.

Larval Hosts: Shrubs in the Laurel family (Lauraceae)—primarily redbays (*Persea* spp.).

Preferred Habitats: Southern swamplands and upland areas that support redbays.

ID Tips: A narrow yellow line runs parallel to the body near the base of the ventral hindwing.

Sulphurs and Whites

Barred Yellow *(Eurema daira)*

Flight Time: Typically late summer and fall in Alabama.

Adult Energy Sources: A variety of small, low-growing flowers.

Larval Hosts: Pea family (Fabaceae), especially pencil-flowers *(Stylosanthes* spp.*)* and joint-vetches (*Aeschynomene* spp.*)*.

Preferred Habitats: Open areas including woodland edges.

ID Tips: Black bar on lower edge of dorsal forewing. Bottom of hindwing is angled rather than rounded.

Note: Generally not a year-round resident in Alabama.

Sleepy Orange *(Eurema niccipe)*

Flight Time: Spring through fall.

Adult Energy Sources: A wide variety of flowers.

Larval Hosts: Pea family (Fabaceae), especially partridge-peas *(Chamaecrista* spp.*)* and sennas *(Senna* spp.*).*

Preferred Habitats: Open areas, during most of the year. In spring, also encountered in woodlands.

ID Tips: Color varies seasonally, but diagonal brown marking on ventral hindwing persists.

Little Yellow *(Pyrisitia lisa)*

Flight Time: Late spring, becoming more common summer through fall.

Adult Energy Sources: A wide variety of flowers.

Larval Hosts: Pea family (Fabaceae), especially partridge-peas *(Chamaecrista* spp.*)* and sennas *(Senna* spp.*).*

Preferred Habitats: Open areas including woodland edges and gardens.

ID Tips: Ventrally, two tiny black dots on hindwing near body.

Clouded Sulphur *(Colias philodice)*

Flight Time: Spring through fall.

Adult Energy Sources: A wide variety of flowers.

Larval Hosts: Pea family (Fabaceae), particularly clovers *(Melilotus* and *Trifolium* spp.*)* and vetches *(Vicia* spp.*).*

Preferred Habitats: Nearly any open weedy site. Favors natural habitats more than Orange Sulphur.

ID Tips: Lemon yellow—no orange scaling.

Note: White ("alba") forms may be indistinguishable from Orange Sulphur in the field.

Orange Sulphur *(Colias eurythema)*

Flight Time: Spring through fall.

Adult Energy Sources: A wide variety of flowers.

Larval Hosts: Pea family (Fabaceae), particularly clovers *(Melilotus* and *Trifolium* spp.*)* and vetches *(Vicia* spp.*).*

Preferred Habitats: Nearly any open weedy site.

ID Tips: Displays at least some orange on forewing. Lacks diagonal brown marking below.

Note: White ("alba") forms may be indistinguishable from Clouded Sulphur in the field.

Southern Dogface *(Zerene cesonia)*

Flight Time: Spring through fall.

Adult Energy Sources: A wide variety of flowers.

Larval Hosts: Pea family (Fabaceae), especially prairie-clovers *(Dalea* spp.*)* and False Indigo *(Amorpha fruticosa).*

Preferred Habitats: Open areas such as weedy fields, prairies, and woodland borders. Not likely to be encountered in gardens or near human habitation.

ID Tips: Distinctly pointed forewing in addition to the "dog's face" on the dorsal forewing that is sometimes visible through closed wings.

Cloudless Sulphur *(Phoebis sennae)*

Flight Time: Spring through fall.

Adult Energy Sources: A wide variety of flowers.

Larval Hosts: Pea family (Fabaceae), especially partridge-peas *(Chamaecrista* spp.*)* and sennas *(Senna* spp.*).*

Preferred Habitats: Open areas including woodland edges and gardens.

ID Tips: Large yellow wings with no black wing edges.

Falcate Orangetip *(Anthocharis midea)*

Flight Time: Spring.

Adult Energy Sources: Small woodland wildflowers including the flowers of its host
plants.

Larval Hosts: Mustard family (Brassicaceae),
particularly toothworts *(Cardamine* spp.*)*
and cresses *(Arabis* spp.*)*.

Preferred Habitats: Woodlands including
bottomlands, especially along borders
and openings.

ID Tips: Hooked or "falcate" forewing tips.
Only male has orange wing tips.

West Virginia White *(Pieris virginiensis)*

Flight Time: Spring.

Adult Energy Sources: Small woodland wildflowers including toothworts *(Cardamine*
spp.*)*.

Larval Hosts: Mustard family (Brassicaceae),
usually toothworts.

Preferred Habitats: Moist, shady mountain
woodlands.

ID Tips: Almost completely white. No spotting. Some gray scaling on wing veins.

Note: Populations are highly localized.

Cabbage White *(Pieris rapae)*

Flight Time: Spring through fall.
Adult Energy Sources: A wide variety of
flowers.
Larval Hosts: Mustard family (Brassicaceae),
primarily cultivated varieties.
Preferred Habitats: Any open sunny habitat.
ID Tips: One (male) or two (female) black
spots of upper forewing. Ventral surfaces
may be either creamy or white.

Checkered White *(Pontia protodice)*

Flight Time: Spring through fall.
Adult Energy Sources: A wide variety of
flowers.
Larval Hosts: Mustard family (Brassicaceae)
including Poorman's Pepperwort *(Lepidium virginicum).*
Preferred Habitats: Open, disturbed areas.
ID Tips: Dorsally, both sexes display black
checks.

Great Southern White *(Ascia monuste)*

Flight Time: Spring through fall.

Adult Energy Sources: A wide variety of
flowers.

Larval Hosts: Mustard family (Brassicaceae)
including saltworts *(Batis* spp.*)* and Poorman's Pepperwort *(Lepidium virginicum).*

Preferred Habitats: Open places near the
coast, including gardens.

ID Tips: Antennal tips are turquoise blue.

Gossamer-Wings

Harvester *(Feniseca tarquinius)*

Flight Time: Spring through fall.

Adult Energy Sources: Nonfloral sources
that reportedly include aphid honey dew.

Larval Hosts: Various species of woolly
aphids.

Preferred Habitats: Woodlands near water.

ID Tips: Ventrally, reddish brown with numerous hindwing spots outlined in white.

Note: Highly erratic when disturbed.

American Copper *(Lycaena phlaeas)*

Flight Time: Spring through fall.

Adult Energy Sources: A variety of small, low-growing flowers.

Larval Hosts: Buckwheat family (Polygonaceae), especially sorrels *(Rumex* spp.*)*.

Preferred Habitats: Open disturbed sites. Not near woodlands.

ID Tips: Ventral forewings orange and gray with dark spots. Hindwings are gray with dark spots and thin, jagged orange border.

Bronze Copper *(Lycaena hyllus)*

Flight Time: Late spring through fall.

Adult Energy Sources: A variety of small, low-growing flowers.

Larval Hosts: Buckwheat family (Polygonaceae). Probably docks *(Rumex* spp.*)*, but species unknown in Alabama.

Preferred Habitats: Early succession, low, wet areas.

ID Tips: Hindwings are gray with dark spots and thick orange border. Nearly twice as large as American Copper.

Note: Not well studied in Alabama.

Great Purple Hairstreak *(Atlides halesus)*

Flight Time: Spring through fall.

Adult Energy Sources: A wide variety of flowers. Especially fond of fall-flowering composites.

Larval Hosts: American Mistletoe *(Phoradendron leucarpum)*, a member of the Christmas Mistletoe family (Viscaceae).

Preferred Habitats: Near woodlands and woodland edges.

ID Tips: Thorax has white spots. Lower abdomen is bright orange.

Coral Hairstreak *(Satyrium titus)*

Flight Time: Late May/June.

Adult Energy Sources: A wide variety of flowers. Particularly fond of Butterfly Milkweed *(Asclepias tuberosa)*.

Larval Hosts: Reportedly Black Cherry *(Prunus serotina)* and wild plums *(Prunus* spp.*)* in the Rose family (Rosaceae).

Preferred Habitats: Openings near woodland edges.

ID Tips: Tailless. Orange spots along outer margins of ventral hindwings. No blue spots.

Edwards' Hairstreak *(Satyrium edwardsii)*

Flight Time: Late May/June.
Adult Energy Sources: A wide variety of
  flowers.
Larval Hosts: Oaks *(Quercus* spp.*)* in the
  Beech family (Fagaceae).
Preferred Habitats: Near oak woodlands.
ID Tips: A band of white ringed oval black
  spots on ventral surface.

Banded Hairstreak *(Satyrium calanus)*

Flight Time: May/early June.
Adult Energy Sources: A wide variety of
  flowers.
Larval Hosts: Oaks *(Quercus* spp.*)* and hickories *(Carya* spp.*)* reported.
Preferred Habitats: Near oak woodlands.
ID Tips: Ventrally, hindwing blue patch not
  capped with red. Band of darkened dashes forms bars.

King's Hairstreak *(Satyrium kingi)*

Flight Time: Late May/June.

Adult Energy Sources: Not well known in Alabama.

Larval Hosts: Horse-Sugar *(Symplocos tinctoria),* a small tree in the Sweet-Leaf family (Symplocaceae).

Preferred Habitats: Hardwood forests, stream margins, and wooded swamps. Tied closely to its host plant.

ID Tips: Prominently orange capped blue patch on ventral hindwing. Central dash on ventral forewing is offset and breaks line of dashes.

Striped Hairstreak *(Satyrium liparops)*

Flight Time: May/early June.

Adult Energy Sources: A wide variety of flowers.

Larval Hosts: In Alabama, confirmed on blueberries *(Vaccinium* spp.*)* in the Heath family (Ericaceae).

Preferred Habitats: Usually near edges of openings of hardwood forests.

ID Tips: Ventral wing bars give impression of stripes. Prominent orange cap on ventral hindwing blue spot.

Oak Hairstreak *(Satyrium favonius)*

Flight Time: May/early June.

Adult Energy Sources: A wide variety of flowers, especially Sparkleberry *(Vaccinium arboreum)*.

Larval Hosts: Oaks *(Quercus* spp.*)*.

Preferred Habitats: Openings near woodland edges.

ID Tips: Jagged line that forms an M (or W) on ventral hindwing near tails. No dorsal blue iridescence.

Note: Subspecies look markedly different.

Juniper Hairstreak *(Callophrys gryneus)*

Flight Time: Spring through fall.

Adult Energy Sources: A wide variety of flowers.

Larval Hosts: Eastern Red-Cedar *(Juniperus virginiana)*, a member of the Cypress family (Cupressaceae).

Preferred Habitats: Open alkaline areas. Also Coastal Red-Cedar stands.

ID Tips: Green. Ventrally forewing band of white is aligned.

Hessel's Hairstreak *(Callophrys hesseli)*

Flight Time: Spring through fall.

Adult Energy Sources: Various small flowers. Not known in Alabama.

Larval Hosts: Atlantic White-Cedar *(Chamaecyparis thyoides)*, a member of the Cypress family (Cupressaceae).

Preferred Habitats: Atlantic White-Cedar Swamps and adjacent woodlands.

ID Tips: Green. Top white spot of ventral forewing band is offset outwardly.

Note: Cross-hatching indicates counties that support Atlantic White-Cedar population and the potential range of Hessel's Hairstreak.

Brown Elfin *(Callophrys augustinus)*

Flight Time: Spring.

Adult Energy Sources: A wide variety of flowers.

Larval Hosts: Primarily plants in the Heath family (Ericaceae).

Preferred Habitats: A variety of acidic habitats.

ID Tips: Small and plain; no frosting or tails.

Frosted Elfin *(Callophrys irus)*

Flight Time: Spring.

Adult Energy Sources: A wide variety of flowers.

Larval Hosts: Pea family (Fabaceae). Lupines *(Lupinus spp.)* and wild indigos *(Baptisia spp.)* reported in other areas.

Preferred Habitats: Clearings in dry oak woods.

ID Tips: Broad ventral hindwing frosting with black spot near tail.

Henry's Elfin *(Callophrys henrici)*

Flight Time: Spring.

Adult Energy Sources: A wide variety of flowers.

Larval Hosts: Depending on subspecies, Hollies *(Ilex spp.)* in the Holly family (Aquifoliaceae); Eastern Redbud *(Cercis canadensis)* in the Pea family (Fabaceae); and probably blueberries *(Vaccinium spp.)* in the Heath family (Ericaceae).

Preferred Habitats: Highly varied.

ID Tips: White marks at upper and lower ends of ventral hindwing dark patch. Short tails.

Eastern Pine Elfin *(Callophrys niphon)*

Flight Time: Spring.

Adult Energy Sources: A wide variety of small flowers.

Larval Hosts: Pine family (Pinaceae).

Preferred Habitats: Typically in the vicinity of sapling pines.

ID Tips: Hindwing has complex and variability colored bands and chevrons. Wing fringes are checkered.

Red-Banded Hairstreak *(Calycopsis cecrops)*

Flight Time: Spring through fall.

Adult Energy Sources: A variety of small flowers.

Larval Hosts: Sumacs (*Rhus* spp.) in the Sumac family (Anacardiaceae), wax-myrtles *(Morella* spp.)* in the Bayberry family (Myricaceae), and oaks *(Quercus* spp.)* in the Beech family (Fagaceae). Often feeds on dead plant material below host.

Preferred Habitats: Woodland edges and adjacent open areas.

ID Tips: On ventral wings, conspicuous orange or red-orange continuous band outwardly edged with black and white. Zigzags on hindwing.

Gray Hairstreak *(Strymon melinus)*

Flight Time: Spring through fall.
Adult Energy Sources: A variety of small
flowers.
Larval Hosts: Food plants represent a variety
of plant families, but the Pea family (Fabaceae) may be most common.
Preferred Habitats: Extremely widespread.
ID Tips: True gray—not gray-brown. The
color is important.

White-M Hairstreak *(Parrhasius m-album)*

Flight Time: Spring through fall.
Adult Energy Sources: A variety of small
flowers.
Larval Hosts: Oaks *(Quercus* spp.*)*, members
of the Beech family (Fagaceae).
Preferred Habitats: Oak woodlands.
ID Tips: Thin white "M" marking on ventral
hindwing. Dorsal wings contain iridescent
blue.

Early Hairstreak *(Erora laeta)*

Flight Time: Reportedly spring and summer.

Adult Energy Sources: None documented in Alabama.

Larval Hosts: Typically, American Beech *(Fagus grandifolia)* in the Beech family (Fagaceae) and possibly Beaked Hazelnut *(Corylus cornuta)*, a member of the Birch family (Betulaceae). Unknown in Alabama.

Preferred Habitats: In or near mature beech forests.

ID Tips: Ventrally, minty-green hindwing with irregular orange band.

Eastern Pygmy-Blue *(Brephidium isopthalma)*

Flight Time: Spring through fall.

Adult Energy Sources: Small flowers, including its host plants.

Larval Hosts: Glassworts *(Salicornia* spp.*)*, members of the Amaranth family (Amaranthaceae) and possibly Saltworts *(Batis* spp.*)* in the Saltwort family (Bataceae).

Preferred Habitats: Salt marshes and adjacent coastal areas.

ID Tips: Tiny brown butterfly. Metallic blue-black hindwing spots near outer margin.

Eastern Tailed-Blue *(Cupido comyntas)*

Flight Time: Spring through fall.
Adult Energy Sources: A variety of flowers.
Larval Hosts: Pea family (Fabaceae), espe-
    cially vetches and clovers.
Preferred Habitats: Open, disturbed sites.
ID Tips: The only blue with tails. Orange
    chevrons are located near tails on both
    ventral and dorsal surfaces.

Spring Azure *(Celastrina ladon)*

Flight Time: Spring.
Adult Energy Sources: A variety of flowers.
Larval Hosts: Primarily dogwoods *(Cornus
    spp.)*, trees in the Dogwood family (Cor-
    naceae).
Preferred Habitats: In or near deciduous
    woodlands.
ID Tips: Ventral wings usually medium gray.
    Dorsal wings often display violet shading
    in the blue. Markings tend to be delicate.
    Typically smaller than Summer Azures.

Summer Azure *(Celastrina neglecta)*

Flight Time: Late spring through fall, although some may emerge earlier in the spring.

Adult Energy Sources: A variety of small flowers.

Larval Hosts: Dogwoods *(Cornus* spp.*)* in the Dogwood family (Cornaceae) and wingstems *(Verbesina* spp.*)* in the Aster family *(Asteraceae)* are verified in Alabama. Probably many others as well.

Preferred Habitats: Open deciduous woodlands—more open areas than other azure species.

ID Tips: Ventral wings whitish to pale gray. Ventral surfaces blue rather than violet. Usually larger than Spring Azures and often more heavily marked.

Appalachian Azure *(Celastrina neglectamajor)*

Flight Time: Late spring/early summer.

Adult Energy Sources: A variety of small flowers.

Larval Hosts: Common Black-Cohosh *(Actaea racemosa)* in the Buttercup family (Ranunculaceae) is the only reported host.

Preferred Habitats: Rich hardwood forests.

ID Tips: Typically largest of the azures. Ventrally pale, dorsally blue, not violet.

Note: Look for host plant to aid in identification.

Silvery Blue *(Glaucopsyche lygdamus)*

Flight Time: Spring.

Adult Energy Sources: Small spring flowers. Especially fond of their host blossoms.

Larval Hosts: Pea family (Fabaceae), primarily Carolina Vetch *(Vicia caroliniana).* Possibly others.

Preferred Habitats: Rich moist deciduous woods.

ID Tips: Row of round white rimmed black spots on ventral wings.

Note: Look for these butterflies when vetches are blooming.

Metalmarks

Little Metalmark *(Calephelis virginiensis)*

Flight Time: Spring through fall.

Adult Energy Sources: Small flowers. Especially fond of yellow composites.

Larval Hosts: Aster family (Asteraceae) members. Vanilla-Leaf *(Carphephorus odoratissimus)* is confirmed in Alabama. May also use Horrid Thistle *(Cirsium horridulum)* since it is confirmed in nearby states.

Preferred Habitats: Pine savannas and flatwoods and open, grassy areas.

ID Tips: Tiny orange butterfly with metallic bands.

Note: Tightly brooded.

Brushfoots

American Snout *(Libytheana carinenta)*

Flight Time: Spring through fall.

Adult Energy Sources: Nonfloral. Nectars infrequently.

Larval Hosts: Hackberries *(Celtis* spp.*),* members of the Elm family (Ulmaceae).

Preferred Habitats: Deciduous woodlands and edges. May occur anywhere when it emigrates.

ID Tips: Elongated palps and squared forewing tip.

Monarch *(Danaus plexippus)*

Flight Time: Spring through fall. Seen mostly during spring and fall migration.

Adult Energy Sources: A variety of flowers including milkweeds *(Asclepias* spp.*).*

Larval Hosts: Milkweeds and other plants within the Milkweed family (Asclepiadaceae).

Preferred Habitats: Sunny open spaces, both natural and disturbed.

ID Tips: Orange with black veins and wide black borders flecked with white dots.

Queen *(Danaus gilippus)*

Flight Time: Summer and fall.

Adult Energy Sources: A variety of flowers including milkweeds *(Asclepias* spp.*).*

Larval Hosts: Milkweeds and other plants within the Milkweed family (Asclepia-daceae), including Gulf Coast Swallow-Wort *(Cynanchum angustifoilium).*

Preferred Habitats: In Alabama, coastal. Sunny open spaces, both natural and disturbed.

ID Tips: Mahogany. White spots extend past the dark border and into the forewings.

Red-Spotted Purple *(Limenitis arthemis astyanax)*

Flight Time: Spring through fall.

Adult Energy Sources: Primarily nonfloral. Occasionally nectars.

Larval Hosts: Black Cherry *(Prunus sero-tina)* in the Rose family (Rosaceae) and willows *(Salix* spp.*)* in the Willow family (Salicaceae) are confirmed in Alabama.

Preferred Habitats: Open woods, forest edges and adjacent open areas.

ID Tips: Black with bright iridescent blue. No tails.

Viceroy *(Limenitis archippus)*

Flight Time: Spring through fall.

Adult Energy Sources: Primarily nonfloral. Occasionally nectars.

Larval Hosts: Willows *(Salix* spp.*)* in the Willow family (Salicaceae) are confirmed in Alabama. Often chooses small trees.

Preferred Habitats: Moist open, shrubby areas.

ID Tips: Strongly resembles the Monarch but has an additional thin black line across its hindwings.

Gulf Fritillary *(Agraulis vanillae)*

Flight Time: Late spring through fall.

Adult Energy Sources: Various flowers.

Larval Hosts: Passion-Flower family (Passifloraceae). Purple Passion-Flower *(Passiflora incarnata)* is a favorite.

Preferred Habitats: Open fields and disturbed sites.

ID Tips: Distinct ventral silver spots.

Zebra Longwing *(Heliconius charithonia)*

Flight Time: Late summer/fall in Alabama.
Adult Energy Sources: Various flowers.
Larval Hosts: Passion-Flower family (Passifloraceae). In Alabama, Yellow Passion-Flower *(Passiflora lutea)* is a favorite.
Preferred Habitats: Woodlands near the coast.
ID Tips: Black and yellow stripes on elongated forewings.

Variegated Fritillary *(Euptoieta claudia)*

Flight Time: Spring through fall.
Adult Energy Sources: Various flowers.
Larval Hosts: Passion-Flower family (Passifloraceae) and violets *(Viola* spp.*)* within the Violet family (Violaceae).
Preferred Habitats: Open fields and disturbed sites.
ID Tips: Ventrally, tawny-orange wings with black spots in forewing and hindwing. No silver spots. Pale-yellow central band.

Diana Fritillary *(Speyeria diana)*

Flight Time: Summer through fall.

Adult Energy Sources: Various flowers, especially thistles *(Cirsium* spp.*)* and milk-weeds *(Asclepias* spp.*)*.

Larval Hosts: Violet species within the Violet family (Violaceae).

Preferred Habitats: Rich deciduous wood-lands and adjacent open areas.

ID Tips: Male: Dorsally, inner three-fifths is black/brown. Wide orange band sur-rounds. Female: Ventrally, hindwing is two-toned blue/brown. No orange on any wing.

Great Spangled Fritillary *(Speyeria cybele)*

Flight Time: Early summer through fall.

Adult Energy Sources: Various flowers. Milkweeds *(Asclepias* spp.*)* and thistles *(Cirsium* spp.*)* are favorites.

Larval Hosts: Violets (*Viola* spp.) within the Violet family (Violaceae).

Preferred Habitats: Open sunny sites.

ID Tips: Ventrally, large metallic silver spots and a wide submarginal yellow band.

Hackberry Emperor *(Asterocampa celtis)*

Flight Time: Spring through fall.
Adult Energy Sources: Primarily nonfloral.
Larval Hosts: Hackberries *(Celtis* spp.*)*, members of the Elm family (Ulmaceae).
Preferred Habitats: Low-lying woods, but also drier upland areas. Parks and yards.
ID Tips: Dorsal forewing tips are dark with a spangling of white dots and a black eyespot.
Note: Appearance is variable.

Tawny Emperor *(Asterocampa clyton)*

Flight Time: Spring through fall.
Adult Energy Sources: Primarily nonfloral.
Larval Hosts: Hackberries *(Celtis* spp.*)*, members of the Elm family (Ulmaceae).
Preferred Habitats: Low-lying woods, but also drier upland areas. Parks and yards.
ID Tips: No white spots or black spot on dorsal forewing. No eyespots on ventral forewing.

American Lady *(Vanessa virginiensis)*

Flight Time: All year.

Adult Energy Sources: Various flowers.

Larval Hosts: Herbs within the Aster family (Asteraceae) known as "everlastings" *(Antennaria* spp. and *Gamochaeta* spp.*).*

Preferred Habitats: Open areas including gardens.

ID Tips: Two large eyespots on ventral hindwing.

Painted Lady *(Vanessa cardui)*

Flight Time: Spring through fall.

Adult Energy Sources: Various flowers.

Larval Hosts: A wide variety of plants especially those in the Aster family (Asteraceae), Mallow family (Malvaceae), and Pea family (Fabaceae). Thistles *(Cirsium* spp.*)* are possibly favorites.

Preferred Habitats: Open areas including gardens.

ID Tips: Four or five small eyespots on ventral hindwing.

Red Admiral *(Vanessa atalanta)*

Flight Time: Spring through fall, possibly all year along the coast.

Adult Energy Sources: Floral and nonfloral sources.

Larval Hosts: Herbs in the Nettle family (Urticaceae).

Preferred Habitats: Usually bare moist woodlands but may be found near any accessible open space.

ID Tips: Dorsal wings have a red-orange forewing band and white forewing spots.

Mourning Cloak *(Nymphalis antiopa)*

Flight Time: All year.

Adult Energy Sources: Nonfloral sources.

Larval Hosts: Birches, willows, elms, and hackberries. Other broad-leaved trees possible. Willows are confirmed in Alabama.

Preferred Habitats: Near deciduous woodlands.

ID Tips: Dorsal wings are dark with bright yellow borders and blue interior spots.

Question Mark *(Polygonia interrogationis)*

Flight Time: All year.

Adult Energy Sources: Primarily nonfloral. Rarely nectars at flowers.

Larval Hosts: Trees within the Elm family (Ulmaceae) and nettles *(Urtica* spp.*)* and false nettles *(Boehmeria* spp.*)* in the Nettle family (Urticaceae).

Preferred Habitats: Deciduous woods with some open space.

ID Tips: Silver-white question mark on ventral hindwing.

Comma Anglewing *(Polygonia comma)*

Flight Time: All year.

Adult Energy Sources: Primarily nonfloral. Rarely nectars at flowers.

Larval Hosts: Nettles and false nettles in the Nettle family (Urticaceae) and trees within the Elm family (Ulmaceae).

Preferred Habitats: Deciduous woods with some open space.

ID Tips: Silvery white comma on ventral hindwing.

Common Buckeye *(Junonia coenia)*

Flight Time: Spring through late fall.
Adult Energy Sources: A variety of flowers.
Larval Hosts: Various herbs within several families including Acanthus (Acanthaceae), Figwort (Scrophulariaceae) in which the false foxgloves *(Agalinis* spp.*)* are often used in Alabama, Plantain (Plantaginaceae) in which both native and exotic plantains are used, and Vervain (Verbenaceae).
Preferred Habitats: A wide variety of open sunny habitats with bare ground.
ID Tips: Dorsally, displays striking, multicolored eyespots on forewings and hindwings.

Baltimore Checkerspot *(Euphydryas phaeton)*

Flight Time: May/June.
Adult Energy Sources: A variety of flowers.
Larval Hosts: Figwort family (Scrophulariaceae) members. False foxglove *(Agalinis* spp.*)* confirmed in Alabama as initial host. Unknown as to whether turtleheads *(Chelone* spp.*)* are also used in this state.
Preferred Habitats: Near oak woods.
ID Tips: Black with red orange patches along both wing margins.

Silvery Checkerspot *(Chlosyne nycteis)*

Flight Time: Spring through fall.

Adult Energy Sources: A variety of flowers.

Larval Hosts: Herbs in the Aster family
(Asteraceae) including sunflowers *(Helian-thus* spp.)*, rosinweeds *(Silphium* spp.)*, and
ragweeds *(Ambrosia* spp.)*.

Preferred Habitats: Open areas.

ID Tips: At least one of the dark spots in the
ventral hindwing band has a white center.
The light band is broken with brown.

Gorgone Checkerspot *(Chlosyne gorgone)*

Flight Time: Unknown in Alabama, possibly
late spring and fall.

Adult Energy Sources: Nectar plants un-known in Alabama. Probably a variety of
flowers.

Larval Hosts: Reportedly various composites
within the Aster family (Asteraceae). Host
unconfirmed in Alabama.

Preferred Habitats: Probably open areas,
particularly disturbed and early succes-sion sites.

ID Tips: Zigzag pattern of brown and white
bands on ventral hindwing.

Texan Crescent *(Anthanassa texana seminole)*

Flight Time: Spring through fall.

Adult Energy Sources: A variety of flowers.

Larval Hosts: Herbs in the Acanthus family (Acanthaceae). Branched Foldwing *(Dicliptera brachiata)* verified in Alabama. Possibly water willows *(Justicia* spp.*)* as well.

Preferred Habitats: Bottomlands and adjacent openings.

ID Tips: Square white marks form a continuous median line on dorsal hindwing.

Phaon Crescent *(Phyciodes phaon)*

Flight Time: Spring through fall.

Adult Energy Sources: A variety of flowers including host plants.

Larval Hosts: Frogfruit *(Phyla* spp.*)*, an herb in the Vervain family (Verbenaceae).

Preferred Habitats: Moist open low-growth areas.

ID Tips: Dorsal pale median forewing band.

Pearl Crescent *(Phyciodes tharos)*

Flight Time: Spring through fall.
Adult Energy Sources: Various flowers.
Larval Hosts: Asters *(Symphyotrichum* spp.*)* within the Aster family (Asteraceae).
Preferred Habitats: Open sunny sites, including gardens.
ID Tips: Hindwing crescent. Extremely variable.

Goatweed Leafwing *(Anaea andria)*

Flight Time: All year.
Adult Energy Sources: Primarily nonfloral.
Larval Hosts: Goatweeds *(Croton* spp.*)*, members of the Spurge family (Euphorbiaceae).
Preferred Habitats: Dry open woods and scrub.
ID Tips: Hooked forewing. Orange dorsal wings. Leaf-like ventral wings. Short tails. Wing edges smooth.

Southern Pearly-Eye *(Lethe portlandia)*

Flight Time: Spring through fall.
Adult Energy Sources: Primarily nonfloral.
Larval Hosts: Canes *(Arundinaria* spp.*)* in the Grass family (Poaceae).
Preferred Habitats: Moist or wet bottomland woods.
ID Tips: Orange antennal clubs.

Northern Pearly-Eye *(Lethe anthedon)*

Flight Time: Late spring through fall.
Adult Energy Sources: Primarily nonfloral.
Larval Hosts: Broad-leaved grasses in the
 Grass family (Poaceae) including River-
 Oats *(Chasmanthium latifolium).*
Preferred Habitats: Moist shady woods.
ID Tips: Antennal clubs are black with orange
 tips.

Creole Pearly-Eye *(Lethe creola)*

Flight Time: Spring through fall.
Adult Energy Sources: Primarily nonfloral.
Larval Hosts: Canes *(Arundinaria* spp.) in the
 Grass family (Poaceae).
Preferred Habitats: Moist or wet bottom-
 land woods.
ID Tips: In ventral forewing, post median line
 pushes outward and forms the shape of
 knuckles in a closed fist.

Appalachian Brown *(Lethe appalachia)*

Flight Time: Late spring through fall.

Adult Energy Sources: Primarily nonfloral.

Larval Hosts: Various sedges *(Carex* spp.*)* in the Sedge family (Cyperaceae).

Preferred Habitats: Moist, shaded or semi-shaded woodlands with a good growth of sedges.

ID Tips: Dorsal forewing is either unspotted or contains only very tiny spots.

Eastern Gemmed-Satyr *(Cyllopsis gemma)*

Flight Time: Early spring through fall.

Adult Energy Sources: Primarily nonfloral. Occasionally visits flowers.

Larval Hosts: Grasses (family Poaceae), especially woodland species.

Preferred Habitats: Openings or edges of deciduous woodlands.

ID Tips: Frosted patch with black spots contains iridescence on ventral hindwing.

Carolina Satyr *(Hermeuptychia sosybius)*

Flight Time: Spring through fall.

Adult Energy Sources: Primarily nonfloral. Occasionally visits flowers.

Larval Hosts: Grasses (family Poaceae), especially woodland species.

Preferred Habitats: A variety of woodland habitats.

ID Tips: Dorsal surfaces plain and unmarked.

Georgia Satyr *(Neonympha areolatus)*

Flight Time: Spring through fall.

Adult Energy Sources: Primarily nonfloral. Occasionally visits flowers.

Larval Hosts: Various sedges *(Carex spp.)* in the Sedge family (Cyperaceae).

Preferred Habitats: Savannas.

ID Tips: Flattened ventral hindwing eyespots within reddish orange lines.

Note: Blend zones may occur, making identification very difficult.

Helicta Satyr *(Neonympha helicta)*

Flight Time: Spring through fall.

Adult Energy Sources: Primarily nonfloral. Occasionally visits flowers.

Larval Hosts: Various sedges *(Carex* spp.*)* in the Sedge family (Cyperaceae).

Preferred Habitats: Typically occurs in more upland habitats than the Georgia Satyr but much more research is needed.

ID Tips: Oval eyespots within reddish-orange lines on ventral hindwing.

Note: Blend zones may occur, making identi-fication very difficult.

Mitchell's Satyr *(Neonympha mitchellii)*

Flight Time: Late May through early September.

Adult Energy Sources: Primarily nonfloral. Occasionally visits flowers.

Larval Hosts: Various sedges *(Carex* spp.*)* in the Sedge family (Cyperaceae).

Preferred Habitats: Primarily beaver-impacted wetlands.

ID Tips: Round eyespots within reddish-orange lines on ventral hindwing. Usually, two to four faint eyespots on ventral forewing.

Note: A Federally Endangered species.

Little Wood-Satyr *(Megisto cymela)*

Flight Time: Spring through fall.

Adult Energy Sources: Primarily nonfloral. Occasionally visits flowers.

Larval Hosts: Grasses (family Poaceae), especially woodland species.

Preferred Habitats: A variety of woodland habitats.

ID Tips: Dorsal and ventral forewings and hindwings have two distinct eyespots.

Note: In south Alabama, some Little Wood-Satyrs may exhibit exceptionally large, bright eyespots. Taxonomically, the wood-satyrs are poorly understood and changes in taxonomy may be on the horizon.

Common Wood Nymph *(Cercyonis pegala)*

Flight Time: Late spring through fall.

Adult Energy Sources: Floral and nonfloral.

Larval Hosts: Grasses (family Poaceae), including bluestem grasses *(Andropogon* spp. and *Schizachyrium* spp.*).*

Preferred Habitats: A variety of open sunny habitats usually near either thickets or tangles, which are used for concealment.

ID Tips: Large yellow forewing patches with two distinct eyespots.

Species That Might Occur in Alabama

The following butterflies are resident in adjacent states, and potentially suitable habitats exist in Alabama. One or more of these species may occur here and should be actively sought.

Hickory Hairstreak *(Satyrium caryaevorus)*

Dusky Azure *(Celastrina nigra)*

Meadow Fritillary *(Boloria bellona)*

Aphrodite Fritillary *(Speyeria aphrodite)*

Green Anglewing *(Poygonia faunus)*

Accidentals and Strays

Records indicate that the following butterflies occasionally find their way to Alabama.

Dainty Sulphur *(Nathalis iole)*

Orange-Barred Sulphur *(Phoebis philea)*

Cassius Blue *(Leptotes cassius)*

Marine Blue *(Leptotes marina)*

Reakirt's Blue *(Echinargus isola)*

Ceraunus Blue *(Hemiargus ceraunus)*

White Peacock *(Anartia jatrophae)*

Counties of Alabama

Organizations

Organizations That Focus on Butterflies

The Lepidopterists' Society
Kelly M. Richers
9417 Carvalho Court
Bakersfield, CA 93311-1846
www.lepsoc.org

North American Butterfly Association
4 Delaware Road
Morristown, NJ 07960
www.naba.org

The Southern Lepidopterists' Society
Jeffrey P. Slotten
5421-NY 69th Lane
Gainesville, FL 32653
www.southernlepsoc.org

Organizations That Focus on Alabama's Native Plants

Alabama Wildflower Society
Margie Anderton
21 County Road 68
Killen, AL 35645
www.alwildflowers.org

Biophilia Nature Association
12695 C.R. 95
Elberta, AL 36530
www.biophilia.net

Conservation Organizations Mentioned in This Book

Alabama Department of Conservation and Natural Resources
64 N. Union Street, Suite 468
Montgomery, AL 36130
www.outdooralabama.com

Alabama Invasive Pest Council
P.O. Box 1454
Auburn, AL 36831-1454
www.se-eppc.org/auburn

National Audubon Society
225 Varick Street
7th Floor
New York, NY 10014
www.audubon.org

The Nature Conservancy—Alabama Field Office
2100 1st Ave. North, Suite 500
Birmingham, AL 35203
www.nature.org/wherewework/northamerica/states/alabama

The Nature Conservancy—Worldwide Office
4245 North Fairfax Drive, Suite 100
Arlington, VA 22203-1606
www.nature.org

Notes

Preface

1. Philip Henry Gosse, *Letters from Alabama: Chiefly Relating to Natural History* (Tuscaloosa: The University of Alabama Press, 1993).

2. Ralph L. Chermock, "Season Summary of North American Lepidoptera for 1952: Southeast," *Journal of the Lepidopterists' Society* 7.3–4 (1953): 102–106.

The Focus

1. Harvester caterpillars are carnivores. However, the woolly aphids they consume are directly tied to specific host-plant species that include beech trees and alders.

2. Philip Henry Gosse, *Letters from Alabama: Chiefly relating to Natural History* (Tuscaloosa: The University of Alabama Press, 1993).

Species Accounts and Family Overviews

1. Philip Henry Gosse, *Letters from Alabama: Chiefly relating to Natural History* (Tuscaloosa: The University of Alabama Press, 1993).

2. Philip Henry Gosse, *Letters from Alabama: Chiefly relating to Natural History* (Tuscaloosa: The University of Alabama Press, 1993).

3. Philip Henry Gosse, *Letters from Alabama: Chiefly relating to Natural History* (Tuscaloosa: The University of Alabama Press, 1993).

4. Kim D. Coder, "Identifying Characteristics of Redbay (*Persea borbonia),*" Outreach Publication SFNR06-4, July 2006. Available at http://www.urbanforestrysouth.org/resources/library/identifying-characteristics-of-redbay-persea-borbonia/file.

5. Rick Cech and Guy Tudor, *Butterflies of the East Coast: An Observer's Guide* (Princeton: Princeton University Press, 2005).

6. Alabama Exotic Pest Council, "Criteria for Evaluating Plant Species for Invasiveness in Alabama." http://www.se-epc.org/Alabama/2007plantlist.pdf.

7. Blanche E. Dean, Amy Mason, and Joab L. Thomas, *Wildflowers of Alabama and Adjoining States* (Tuscaloosa: The University of Alabama Press, 1973).

8. NatureServe is a nonprofit conservation organization whose mission is to provide the scientific basis for effective conservation action.

9. NatureServe Explorer: An online encyclopedia of life [Web application]. Version 7.0, 2008. NatureServe, Arlington, VA. U.S.A. Available at http://www.natureserve.org/explorer.

10. H. E. LeGrand and T. E. Howard, *Notes on the Butterflies of North Carolina—Sixteenth Approximation,* March 2009. Available at http://www.ncsparks.net/butterfly/nbnc.html.

11. Thomas C. Emmel, *Florida's Fabulous Butterflies* (Tampa: World Publications, 1997).

12. Robert Frost, *The Poetry of Robert Frost: The Collected Poems, Complete and Unabridged,* ed. Edward Connery Latham (New York: Henry Holt and Company, 1969), 225.

13. Philip Henry Gosse, *Letters from Alabama: Chiefly relating to Natural History* (Tuscaloosa: The University of Alabama Press, 1993).

14. Philip Henry Gosse, *Letters from Alabama: Chiefly relating to Natural History* (Tuscaloosa: The University of Alabama Press, 1993).

15. Quoted in Mart A. Stewart, "From King Cane to King Cotton: Razing Cane in the Old South," *Environmental History* 12.1 (2007): 29 pars. Available at http://www.historycooperative.org/journals/eh/12.1/stewart.html.

16. Philip Henry Gosse, *Letters from Alabama: Chiefly relating to Natural History* (Tuscaloosa: The University of Alabama Press, 1993).

17. John Henry Comstock and Anna Botsford Comstock, *How to Know the Butterflies* (New York: D. Appleton and Company, 1913).

18. Will Cook, "Carolina Satyr (Hermeuptychia sosybius)," North American Butterfly Nature Photos. Available at http://www.carolinanature.com.html.

19. Philip Henry Gosse, *Letters from Alabama: Chiefly relating to Natural History* (Tuscaloosa: The University of Alabama Press, 1993).

20. Samuel Hubbard Scudder, *Everyday Butterflies: A Group of Biographies.* Boston: Houghton, Mifflin and Company, 1899.

Focus on the Future

1. Wildlife and Freshwater Fisheries Division, "Conserving Alabama's Wildlife: A Comprehensive Strategy." Alabama Department of Conservation and Natural Resources, Montgomery, Alabama.

Glossary

Abdomen. The portion of the body located behind the thorax.

Acetogenin. Chemical compounds with antitumor properties found in pawpaws.

Aestivate. To spend periods of the summer in an inactive state.

Aka. Also known as.

Alba. White.

Alien. Not native.

Alkaloid. A member of a large group of chemicals that are made by plants. Many possess potent pharmacologic properties.

Androconia. Specialized scales that produce pheromones for mate attraction. Found in the males of several groups, they are often located in patches along hindwing veins.

Anglewing. A butterfly in the genus Polygonia (which means "many angled").

Ant-tended. Protected by specific species of ants.

Antenna(-nae). Long, sensory appendage that is attached from the top of the head.

Antennal club. Enlarged tip of an antenna.

Antioxidant. A chemical compound or substance that inhibits oxidation.

Aposematic. Conspicuous or warning colors indicative of a special means of defense against predators.

Aristocholic acid. Derived from Aristolochia (Pipevine) plants.

Avian. Pertaining to birds.

Bask. To expose the dorsal wing surface to the sun's rays to obtain heat energy.

Blackland prairie. Grasslands occurring in areas with calcareous bedrock. Consists of prairie islands surrounded by forest. Only remnants remain in the Alabama Black Belt.

Blend zone. An area where two or more species intermingle and interbreed.

Bract. A modified or specialized leaf.

Broad leaved. Trees without needles. Deciduous trees, shrubs, and vines.

Brood. One generation of a species.

Byre. A detritus structure built by ants. Literally, "cow shed."

Calcium oxalate. A poisonous, colorless crystalline organic acid found in many plants. Used as a bleach and rust remover.

Camouflage. Concealment by disguise or protective coloring.

Canebrake. A dense thicket of cane.

Canopy. The uppermost layer in a forest, formed by the crowns of the trees.

Cardiac glycoside. Any of several glycosides obtained chiefly from plant sources such as the foxglove, used medicinally to increase the force of contraction of heart muscle and to regulate heartbeats.

Carrion. The carcass of a dead animal.

Catkin. A dense, cylindrical, often drooping cluster of unisexual flowers found in willows, birches, and oaks.

Cedar glade. Natural opening where limestone bedrock is at or near the soil surface and in which climax vegetation is a mixture of grasses, annuals, and perennials. The term "cedar" references the Eastern Red-cedars that typically inhabit adjacent woods.

Chitin. A tough, protective, semitransparent substance forming the principal component of arthropod exoskeletons.

Chlorophyll. A green pigment found in most plants.

Chrysalis (-ises or -ides). A hard case where a caterpillar transforms into an adult. A pupa.

Coastal Plain. The extensive geologically and ecologically variable region southeast of the Piedmont.

Communal. Grouping together.

Complete metamorphosis. Passing through four distinct stages of development: egg, larva, pupa, adult.

Composites. Plants within the Aster family (Asteraceae).

Compound. In chemistry, a substance consisting of two or more different elements bonded together in a fixed mass ratio that can be split into simpler substances.

Conifer. Any of various mostly needle leaved or scale leaved, chiefly evergreen, cone-bearing trees or shrubs such as pines.

Coniferous. Referring to softwoods—in Alabama, usually pines.

Countershading. Protective coloration in an animal or insect, characterized by darker coloring of areas exposed to light and lighter coloring of areas that are normally shaded.

Cove forest. A type of deciduous forest community associated with the Appalachian Mountains. Found in protected positions in the landscape at middle to low elevations and typified by high species richness of both plants and animals.

Crepuscular. Becoming active at twilight or before sunrise.

Crucifer. A plant in the Mustard family *(Brassicaceae).*

Crypsis. The ability of an organism to avoid observation.

Cryptic. Blending into the environment.

Culm. A cane stem.

Danaid. A group of butterflies that use milkweeds as their larval hosts. In Alabama, Monarchs and Queens.

Danaidone. A pheromone.

Deciduous. Woody plants that drop their leaves during winter.

Defense mechanism. A self-protective reaction by an organism.

Detritus. Material from decaying plants.

Diapause. A period of delayed or halted development during any life stage. Usually results from environmental stress.

Dicotyledon. Any flowering plant that produces two leaves on its first shoot from seed.

Dimorphic. Having two distinct forms.

Disturbed site. Habitat created by some type of disruption.

Dormant. Inactive.

Dorsal. The upper surface.

Dry season. Occurs in winter months in Alabama and is typified by less rainfall and cooler temperatures.

Duff. The partly decayed organic matter on the forest floor.

Early succession. The early stages of plant succession are composed of species capable of colonizing bare ground. These plant species flourish initially, but soon decline as the bare ground diminishes from plant occupation.

Eclose. To emerge.

Ecosystem. The complex of a community of organisms and its environment functioning as an ecological unit.

Edge. The overlap where one habitat ends and another begins.

Emigrant. One who leaves a place of residence to live somewhere else.

Emigrate. Leaving a place of residence to live somewhere else.

Ericad. A member of the Heath family (Ericaceae). Shrubby, often evergreen plants that thrive on open barren usually acid soil.

Ethereal oil. A concentrated, water-repellant liquid containing volatile aroma from plants.

Everlastings. Any of several chiefly composite plants such as pussytoes with flowers that can be dried without loss of form or color.

Extrafloral nectary. Special organs within plants that secrete a substance relished by ants.

Eyespots. The rings on a butterfly wing that resemble eyes.

Falcate. Hooked. Usually refers to a wing tip.

Fall line. The area where the upland region meets the Coastal Plain. Probably the most important physical feature in Alabama affecting the distribution of plants and animals.

Family. A group with many similar characteristics.

Federally endangered. Species that meet the requirements for protection of the Federal Endangered Species Act of 1973.

Flatwoods. A woodland in a low-lying region having little drainage

Floodplain. Level land that may be submerged by floodwaters.

Fluorescence. Light emission.

Forelegs. The first pair of legs behind a butterfly's head.

Forewing. The pair of wings closest to the head.

Form. A color, seasonal, or geographic variation of a species.

Frass. Caterpillar excrement or droppings.

Fugitive species. A species adapted to colonize newly disturbed habitats.

Furanocoumarin. Naturally occurring substances in plants that produce a toxic reaction to light. Many furanocoumarins are toxic and are produced by plants as a defense mechanism against various types of predators.

Generation. The average span of time between the birth of parents and that of their offspring.

Genus. The category of biological classification that ranks between the family and the species. Usually further divided into several subordinate species.

Glucosinolate. Substances occurring widely in plants of the genus *Brassica;* broken down by an enzyme to yield, among other products, the mustard oils which are responsible for the pungent flavor (especially in mustards).

Glycerol. A syrupy, sweet, colorless or yellowish liquid obtained from fats and oils and used as a solvent, antifreeze, plasticizer, and sweetener.

Glycoside. An herbal carbohydrate that exerts a powerful effect on hormone-producing tissues.

Granite outcrop. Exposed granite bedrock surfaces that support unique assemblages of plants and animals.

Gravid. Carrying developing eggs.

Greater fritillary. Butterflies belonging to genus Speyeria.

Gregarious. Grouped together.

Habitat. The ecological community in which an organism lives.

Habitat generalist. Accepting a wide variety of living conditions.

Habitat specialist. Accepting only very limited living conditions.

Hairpencil. A hair-like structure on the legs or abdomens of some butterflies and moths that aids in the distribution of pheromones during courtship.

Hard pine. A pine (such as longleaf pine or pitch pine) that has hard wood and leaves usually in groups of two or three.

Heath. Any member of the Heath family (Ericaceae). Shrubby, often evergreen plants that thrive on open barren usually acid soil.

Heliconia. A genus of butterflies often called "Longwings."

Herbaceous. Referring to deciduous plants without woody stems.

Herbivore. An organism that eats plants.

Herbivory. Eating plants.

Hibernaculum. A winter shelter (usually a rolled leaf) for an insect.

Hilltopping. Mate-location behavior in which males and unmated females fly to the highest geographical point. Males often establish and defend territories.

Hindwing. The rear wings, farthest from the head.

Host. A plant or other organism fed upon by larvae.

Immigrant. An individual that moves to an area from somewhere else.

Inflorescence. A flower cluster.

Instar. A single stage of caterpillar development. Butterfly larvae go through four to eight instars depending on species.

Introduced. Alien or exotic species living outside their native distributional range as a result of human activity. Some introductions have been intentional; others were accidental.

Iridoid glycoside. Chemical compounds found primarily in asters (Asteridae).

Labial palp. The elongated mouthpart that lies on either side of the proboscis.

Larva (-ae). Developmental stage that occurs between the egg and the pupa. It is the eating phase. Butterfly larvae are known as caterpillars.

Legume. A plant in the pea family.

Lepidopterist. A person who studies butterflies and moths.

Limbing up. Cutting off the lower branches of a plant.

Longwing. Butterflies within the genus Heliconia.

Lupanine. A bitter crystalline poisonous alkaloid found in various lupines.

Margin. The wing edge.

Mayolene. Insecticidal oils found on the tips of some pierid body hairs.

Migrant. One that moves from one region to another by chance, instinct, or plan.

Migrate. To travel from one region to another and at least begin the return trip.

Mimic. An impersonator.

Mimicry. Copying another through appearance or behavior.

Mimicry ring. A group of species that all mimic the same pattern.

Molt. To shed the skin or exoskeleton.

Monocotyledon. A flowering plant with a single leaf from its initial sprout. Includes grasses and sedges.

Monoculture. The cultivation of a single crop on a farm or in a region. One homogeneous culture without diversity.

Multivoltine. Completing two or more generations annually.

Mustard oil. This oil has a strong smell and a hot nutty taste. Gives mustard its characteristics flavor and aroma.

Myrmecophily. Associated with or benefited by ants.

Naturalized. Introduced from another region but persists without cultivation.

Nectar. *n.* A sweet liquid secreted by plants as food to attract animals that will benefit them. *v.* The act of sipping nectar from a flower.

Nectarer. An organism that sips nectar.

Nectary. A gland-like organ, located outside or within a flower that secretes nectar.

Nigra. Dark or black.

Nitrogen-fixing. The conversion of atmospheric nitrogen into compounds that plants and other organisms can assimilate. The majority of nitrogen-fixing plants are in the Legume family.

Osmeterium (-ia). An eversible gland on the first thoracic segment of some caterpillars that secretes a foul-smelling substances to ward off predators.

Overwinter. To pass through the winter season.

Oviposit. To lay eggs.

Ovum (-va). An egg.

Oxalic acid. A poisonous, colorless crystalline organic acid found in many plants, such as spinach, and used as a bleach and rust remover.

PA. Abbreviation for pyrrolizidine alkaloids.

Palp. A sensory appendage located near the mouth.

Parasite. An organism that grows, feeds, and is sheltered on or in a different organism while contributing nothing to the survival of its host.

Patrol. To actively search for mates while flying back and forth through an area.

Perch. To station oneself on a leaf or twig to search for mates.

Petiole. The stalk by which a leaf is attached to a stem.

Pheromone. A chemical secreted by an animal, especially an insect, that influences the behavior or development of others of the same species, often functioning as an attractant of the opposite sex.

Photoperiod. The amount of hours in a day where the environment is either light or dark.

Phytochemical. Non-nutrient plant chemicals that contain protective, disease-preventing compounds.

Pierid. Any butterfly from the genus Pieris.

Pinnately compound. Leaflets arranged in two rows along an axis.

Pollen. A mass of male spores in a seed plant appearing usually as a fine dust.

Predator. A carnivorous animal.

Proboscis (-cises). An elongated appendage from the head used for tubular feeding and sucking.

Pteridine. A yellow crystalline base that is a structural constituent of various animal pigments.

Puddle. To sip from wet spots.

Puddle club. A gathering of butterflies (usually males) at wet spots.

Pupa (-ae). The nonfeeding stage between the larva and adult in insect metamorphosis during which the larva undergoes complete transformation within a protective cocoon or hardened case.

Pupation. The process in which a larva undergoes complete transformation within a protective cocoon or hardened case.

Pyrrolizidine alkaloids. Liver-damaging toxins found in plants primarily within the Fabaceae, Asteraceae, and Boraginaceae families.

Reproductive diapause. A period during which reproduction and reproductive activities are suspended, generally due to adverse environmental conditions.

Rosa. Tinged with pink or red.

Samara. A winged, typically one-seeded fruit.

Sandhills. Islands of exposed sand and sparse vegetation in the midst of denser forest, found along the northern and eastern banks of large Coastal Plain streams in Alabama.

Satyrium. A genus of hairstreaks.

Savanna. A flat, grass-covered area of tropical or subtropical regions, nearly treeless in some places but generally having a mix of widely spaced trees and bushes.

Scent patches. Androconia. Specialized scales that produce pheromones for mate attraction. Found in the males of several groups, they are often located in patches along hindwing veins.

Secrete. To generate and expel a substance from cells or bodily fluids.

Sedentary. Not moving.

Sepal. One of the usually separate, green parts that surround and protect the flower bud and extend from the base of a flower after it has opened.

Species. A class of individuals having common attributes and designated by a common name.

Species of Special Concern. Life forms that should be closely monitored because threats to habitat, their limited distribution, and/or specific life history requirements may cause them to be threatened or endangered within the foreseeable future.

Spermatophore. A compact mass of sperm cells extruded by the males and directly transferred to the reproductive parts of the female.

Stamen. The pollen-bearing male part of a flower.

Subfamily. A subdivision of the taxonomic group family.

Subspecies. A taxonomic subdivision of a species consisting of an interbreeding, usually geographically isolated population of organisms.

Substrate. A surface on which an organism grows or is attached.

Succession. An ecological process in which one plant community replaces another over time.

Taxonomist. A biologist who specializes in the classification of organisms into groups on the basis of their structure and origin and behavior.

Taxonomy. The orderly classification of plants and animals according to their pre-sumed natural relationships.

Temperate. Characterized by moderate temperatures, weather, or climate.

Thermoregulation. Maintenance of a constant internal body temperature indepen-dent from the environmental temperature.

Thoracic. Located on or near the thorax.

TILS. The International Lepidoptera Survey, a nonprofit organization devoted to the discovery, determination, and documentation of new butterflies and moths around the world.

Tribe. A taxonomic classification that groups several species into a single category.

Tropical. Characterized by a hot, equator-like climate.

Tubercle. A small rounded projecting part or outgrowth.

Ultraviolet. Beyond the rays of the violet end of the visible light spectrum. Has short-er wavelengths than visible light.

Understory. An underlying layer of vegetation, especially the plants that grow be-neath a forest's canopy.

Univoltine. Single brooded.

Uric acid. A chemical created when the body breaks down substances.

Vaccinium. A genus of ericaceous shrubs including the various kinds of blueberries.

Venation. A pattern of veins.

Ventral. The under or lower surface.

Waste areas. Uncultivated, highly disturbed sites.

Watershed. The region draining into a river, river system, or other body of water.

Wet season. The rainy season covering one or more months when most of the aver-age annual rainfall in a region occurs.

Resources

Books about Butterflies

Allen, Thomas J. *The Butterflies of West Virginia and Their Caterpillars.* Pittsburgh: University of Pittsburgh Press, 1997.

Allen, Thomas J., Jim Brock, and Jeffrey Glassberg. *Caterpillars in the Field and Garden: A Field Guide to the Butterfly Caterpillars of North America.* Oxford: Oxford University Press, 2005.

Brock, Jim P., and Kenn Kaufman. *Butterflies of North America* (Kaufman Field Guides). Boston: Houghton Mifflin Company, 2003.

Cech, Rick, and Guy Tudor. *Butterflies of the East Coast: An Observer's Guide.* Princeton, N.J.: Princeton University Press, 2005.

Comstock, John Henry, and Anna Botsford Comstock. *How to Know the Butterflies.* New York: D. Appleton and Company, 1913.

Emmel, Thomas C. *Florida's Fabulous Butterflies.* Tampa: World Publications, 1997.

Feltwell, John. *The Natural History of Butterflies.* New York: Facts on File Publications, 1986.

Glassberg, Jeffrey. *Butterflies through Binoculars: The East* (Butterflies through Binoculars Series). New York: Oxford University Press, 1999.

Glassberg, Jeffrey, Marc C. Minno, and John V. Calhoun. *Butterflies through Binoculars: A Field, Finding, and Gardening Guide to Butterflies in Florida* (Butterflies through Binoculars Field Guide Series). New York: Oxford University Press, 2000.

Harris, Lucien, Jr. *Butterflies of Georgia.* Norman: University of Oklahoma Press, 1972.

Holland, W. J. *The Butterfly Book.* New York: Doubleday, Page and Company, 1898.

Klots, Alexander B. *A Field Guide to the Butterflies: North America East of the Great Plains* (Peterson Field Guide Series). Boston: Houghton Mifflin Company, 1951.

Miller, Jacqueline Y., ed. *The Common Names of North American Butterflies.* Washington, D.C.: Smithsonian Institute Press, 1992.

Miller, Jeffrey C., Daniel H. Janzen, and Winifred Hallwachs. *100 Butterflies and Moths.* Cambridge, Mass.: The Belknap Press of Harvard University Press, 2007.

Minno, Marc C., Jerry F. Butler, and Donald W. Hall. *Florida Butterfly Caterpillars and Their Host Plants.* Gainesville: University of Florida Press, 2005.

O'Donnell, Jane E., Lawrence F. Gall, and David L. Wagner, eds. *The Connecticut Butterfly Atlas.* Hartford, Conn.: State Geological and Natural History Survey, 2007.

Opler, Paul O., and George O. Krizek. *Butterflies: East of the Great Plains.* Baltimore: John Hopkins University Press, 1984.

Opler, Paul O., and Vichai Malikul. *A Field Guide to Eastern Butterflies* (Peterson Field Guide Series). Boston: Houghton Mifflin Company, 1992.

Schappert, Phil. *A World for Butterflies: Their Lives, Behaviour, and Future.* Buffalo: Firefly Books, 2000.

Scott, J. A. *The Butterflies of North America: A Natural History and Field Guide.* Stanford: Stanford University Press, 1986.

Scriber, J. Mark, Yoshitaka Tsubaki, and Robert C. Lederhouse, eds. *Swallowtail Butterflies: Their Ecology and Evolutionary Biology.* Gainesville, Fla.: Scientific Publishers, 1995.

Scudder, Samuel Hubbard. *Everyday Butterflies: A Group of Biographies.* Boston: Houghton, Mifflin and Company, 1899.

Tveten, John, and Gloria Tveten. *Butterflies of Houston and Southeast Texas.* Austin: University of Texas Press, 1996.

Tyler, Hamilton A. *Swallowtail Butterflies of North America.* Healdsburg, Calif.: Naturegraph Publishers, 1975.

Wagner, David L. *Caterpillars of Eastern North America: A Guide to Identification and Natural History* (Princeton Field Guides). Princeton, N.J.: Princeton University Press, 2005.

Books about Plants

Dean, Blanche E. *Trees and Shrubs in the Heart of Dixie.* Birmingham: Coxe Publishing Company, 1961.

Dean, Blanche E., Amy Mason, and Joab L. Thomas. *Wildflowers of Alabama and Adjoining States.* Tuscaloosa: The University of Alabama Press, 1973.

Hemmerly, Thomas E. *Wildflowers of the Central South.* Nashville: Vanderbilt University Press, 1990.

Ladd, Doug. *Tallgrass Prairie Wildflowers: A Field Guide.* Helena, Mt.: Falcon Publishing, 1995.

Minno, Marc C., and Maria Minno. *Florida Butterfly Gardening.* Gainesville: University Press of Florida, 1999.

Murdy, William H., and M. Eloise Brown Carter. *Guide to the Plants of Granite Outcrops.* Athens: University of Georgia Press, 2000.

Vanderplank, John. *Passion Flowers.* Cambridge, Mass.: MIT Press, 2000.

Zomlefer, Wendy B. *Guide to the Flowering Plant Families.* Chapel Hill: University of North Carolina Press, 1994.

Books about Alabama

Gosse, Philip Henry. *Letters from Alabama: Chiefly Relating to Natural History.* Tuscaloosa: The University of Alabama Press, 1993.

Journals, Periodicals, and Reports

Angevine, Mark W., and Peter Brussard. "Population Structure and Gene Frequency Analysis of Sibling Species of Lethe." *Journal of the Lepidopterists' Society* 33.1 (1979): 29–36.

Berenbaum, May R. "Aposematism and Mimicry in Caterpillars." *Journal of the Lepidopterists' Society* 49.4 (1995): 386–396.

Bowers, Deane. "Observations on *Erora Laeta* (Lycaenidae) in New Hampshire." *Journal of the Lepidopterists' Society* 32.2 (1978): 140.

Chermock, Ralph L. "Season Summary of North American Lepidoptera for 1952: Southeast." *Journal of the Lepidopterists' Society* 7.3–4 (1953): 102–106.

Einem, Gerald E. "Attraction of Male Queen Butterflies to Cardenolide—and Alkaloid—Containing Plants During Fall Migrations." *News of the Lepidopterists' Society* 46.3 (2004): 94–97.

Gatrelle, R. R. "An Evolutionary Subspecific Assessment of *Deciduphagus henrici* (Lycaenidae) Based on Its Utilization of Ilex and non-Ilex Hosts." *The Taxonomic Report, The International Lepidoptera Survey* 6 (1999): 1–10.

———"An Examination of Southeastern U.S. Satyrium (Lycaenidae: Theclinae). Part One: An Obscure New Species of Satyrium edwardsii." *The Taxonomic Report, The International Lepidoptera Survey* 2 (2001).

——— "Hubner's Helicta: The Forgotten Neonympha." *The Taxonomic Report, The International Lepidoptera Survey* 8 (1999).

———"Notes of the Confusion between Lethe Creola and Lethe Portlandia (Satyridae)." *Journal of the Lepidopterists' Society* 25.2 (1971): 145–146.

———"The Rediscovery, Taxonomy, and Biology of Chlosyne gorgone gorgone and Chlosyne ismeria (Nymphlidae) in Burke County, Georgia." *The Taxonomic Report, The International Lepidoptera Survey* 2 (1998).

———"Taxonomic Analysis of the Genus Megisto (Satyridae) in the Eastern United States." *The Taxonomic Report, The International Lepidoptera Survey* 5 (2005).

Hart, Barry. "A Survey for the Mitchell's Satyr (*Neonympha mitchellii* FRENCH) in the National Forest of Alabama (Final Report)." June 2004.

James, David G. "Comparative Studies of the Immature Stages and Development Biology of Five Argynnis spp. (Subgenus Speyeria) (Nymphalidae) from Washington." *Journal of the Lepidopterists' Society* 62 (2008): 61–70.

Pavulaan, Harry. "The Biology, Life History, and Taxonomy of *Celastrina neglectamajor* (Lycaenidae: Polyommantinae)." *The Taxonomic Report* 2 (2000).

Pavulaan, Harry, and D. M. Wright. "*Pterourus appalachiensis* (Papilionidae: Papilioninae), a New Swallowtail Butterfly from the Appalachian Region of the United States." *The Taxonomic Report* 7 (2002).

Ross, Gary Noel. "Monarch Section." *Louisiana Wildlife Federation* 4 (2001): 13–40.

Smedley, Scott R., F. C. Schroeder, D. B. Weibel, J. Meinwald, K. A. Lafleur, J. A. Renwick, R. Rutowski, and T. Eisner. "Mayolenes: Labile Defensive Lipids from the Glandular Hairs of a Caterpillar (Pieris rapae)." *PNAS* 99.10 (May 14, 2002): 6822–6827.

Sullivan, Bolling. "Captures of *Erora Laeta* in North Carolina (Lycaenidae)." *Journal of the Lepidopterists' Society* 25.4 (1971): 295.

Webster, R. P., and M. C. Nielson. "Myrmecophily in the Edward's Hairstreak Butterfly *Satyrium edwardsii* (Lycaenidae)." *Journal of the Lepidopterists' Society* 38.2 (1984): 124–133.

Wildlife and Freshwater Fisheries Division, Alabama Department of Conservation and Natural Resources. "Conserving Alabama's Wildlife: A Comprehensive Strategy." Alabama Department of Conservation and Natural Resources, Montgomery, Alabama.

Web Sites and Electronic Media

Coder, Kim D. "Identifying Characteristics of Redbay *(Persea borbonia)."* Outreach Publication SFNR06-4, July 2006. At http://www.urbanforestrysouth.org/resources/library/identifying-characteristics-of-redbay-persea-borbonia/file<ul>_</ul>name.

Kirk, Kathryn. Conservation Assessment of Henry's Elfin *Butterfly (Callophrys henrici)*. USDA Forest Service, Eastern Region. Available at http://www.fs.fed.us/r9/wildlife/tes/ca-overview/docs/insect<ul>_</ul>callophrys<ul>_</ul>henrici-HenrysElfinButterfly.pdf.

LeGrand, H. E., and T. E. Howard. *Notes on the Butterflies of North Carolina—Sixteenth Approximation,* March 2009. At http://www.ncsparks.net/butterfly/nbnc.html.

NatureServe. NatureServe Explorer: An online encyclopedia of life [Web application]. Version 7.0, 2008. NatureServe, Arlington, Virginia. Available at http://www.natureserve.org/explorer.

Opler, Paul A., Harry Pavulaan, Ray E. Stanford, and Michael Pogue, coordinators. *Butterflies and Moths of North America.* Bozeman, Mt.: Big Sky Institute, 2006. Available at http://www.butterfliesandmoths.org/.

Shepherd, M. D. "Species Profile: *Callophrys irus.*" In Shepherd, M. D., D. M. Vaughan, and S. H. Black (eds.), *Red List of Pollinator Insects of North America.* CD-ROM Version 1 (May 2005). Portland, Ore.: The Xerces Society for Invertebrate Conservation, 2005.

Stewart, Mart A. "From King Cane to King Cotton: Razing Cane in the Old South." *Environmental History* 12.1 (2007): 29 pars. Available at http://www.historycooperative.org/journals/eh/12.1/stewart.html.

USDA, NRCS. The PLANTS Database (http://plants.usda.gov, February 23, 2009). National Plant Data Center, Baton Rouge, Louisiana, 70874-4490 USA.

Warren, A. D., K. J. Davis, N. V. Grishin, J. P. Pelham, and E. M. Stangeland. Interactive Listing of American Butterflies. [15-II-09]. Available at http://www.butterfliesofamerica.com/.

Index

camouflage, 6, 9, 19, 21, *22*, 25, *35*, 42, 59, 60, 66, 71, 74, 90, 105, 123, *125*, 128, *134*, 136, 144, *155*, 158, *159*, *173*, 184, 190, 215, 216, 218, 255, *278*, *284*, 295, 340, 348, 352, 356, 370, 379

cane, 345, 347, 348, 352, 441, 442; Giant, *344, 346, 352, 354, 355*, 401; Switch, 345, 352, 403

canebrake, 345, 352

cardiac glycoside. *See* glycoside: cardiac

Cardinal-Flower, *88,* 90, 400

Carolina Mantis, 402. *See also* praying mantis

Carolina Redroot, 158, 400

Carolina Satyr. *See* satyr: Carolina

Carolina Vetch, *206, 207,* 400, 428

Carpet Grass. *See* grass: Carpet

Carphephorus odoratissimus. *See* Vanilla-Leaf

caraway, 28

Carrot/Parsley family (Apiaceae), 17, 28, 400, 406

Carya. *See* hickory

Cassius Blue. *See* blue: Cassius

Ceanothus americanus. *See* Common New Jersey-Tea

Cech, Rick, 63

cedar glade, 154

Celastrina: *C. ladon* (*see* azure: Spring); *C. neglecta* (*see* azure: Summer); *C. neglecta-major* (*see* azure: Appalachian); *C. nigra (*see* azure: Dusky)

Celtis: *C. laevigata* (*see* Sugarberry). *See also* hackberry

Cercis canadensis. *See* redbud: Eastern

Cercyonis pegala. *See* Common Wood Nymph

Chamaecrista: *C. facsiculata* (*see* partridge-pea: Common). *See* partridge-pea

Chamaecyparis thyoides. *See* Atlantic White-Cedar

Chasmanthium: *C. latifolium* (*see* River-Oats); *C. laxum* (*see* grass: Slender Spikegrass)

Checkered White. *See* white: Checkered

checkerspot, 216, 325; Baltimore, *316–19*, 438; Gorgone, xiv, *324–27*, 439; Silvery, *320–23*, 439

Chelone. *See* turtlehead

Chermock, Ralph, xiii, 356, 393

Chinese Mustard: *See* mustard: Chinese

Chinese Privet. *See* privet: Chinese

Chinese Tallow-Tree, 395, 400

Chlosyne: *C. gorgone* (*see* checkerspot: Gorgone); *C. nycteis* (*see* checkerspot: Silvery)

Cimicifuga racemosa. *See* Common Black-Cohosh

Cirsium horridulum. *See* thistle: Horrid

Citrus family or Citrus/Rue family (Rutaceae), 17, 37, 400, 407

Cleburne County, 324

Climbing Hempvine, 134, 400

Clouded Sulphur. *See* sulphur: Clouded

Cloudless Sulphur. *See* sulphur: Cloudless

clover, 74, 82, 84, 182, 192, 400, 411, 426; Crimson, 400; Gattinger's

Edwards' Hairstreak. *See* hairstreak: Edwards'

elfin: Brown, 160–63, *161, 162, 163,* 421; Eastern Pine, 172–75, 423; Frosted, 164–67, *165, 166, 167,* 422; Henry's, 164, *168–71,* 422

elm, 436, 438; family (Ulmaceae), 303, 400, 429, 434, 437; Winged, *302, 303, 304, 306, 307, 310,* 404

Elymus hystrix. See grass: Eastern Bottlebrush

Emmel, Thomas, 182

emperor, 216; Hackberry, 5, *276–79,* 280, 434; Tawny, 5, *280–85,* 434

Endangered Species Act, 394; federally endangered, 378, 445

Enodia. See Lethe

Ericaceae. *See* heath: family

Erigeron. See Daisy Fleabane

Erora laeta. See hairstreak: Early

Escambia County, 156

Euonymus atropurpureus. See American Wahoo

Eupatorium. See Thoroughwort

Euphydryas phaeton. See checkerspot: Baltimore

Euptoieta claudia. See fritillary: Variegated

Eurema: *E. daira* (*see* sulphur: Barred Yellow); *E. nicippe* (*see* sulphur: Sleepy Orange)

Eurytides marcellus. See swallowtail: Zebra

Fagus grandifolia. See American Beech

Falcate Orangetip, 5, *94–97,* 413

False Foxglove, *315, 317,* 400, 438

False Indigo. *See* indigo: False

False Nettle. *See* nettle: False

Feniseca tarquinius. See Harvester

Fennel, 28

Figwort family (Scrophulariaceae), 312, 317, 400, 438

Finkelstein, Irving, 169

fire/fire suppression, 156, 164, 370, 380, 394. *See also* controlled burn

fire ant. *See* ant: fire

Florida, 37, 88, 110, 151, 155, 156, 158, 160, 164, 251, 252, 328, 330, 356, 386

Flowering Dogwood. *See* dogwood: Flowering

Fluted Swallowtail. *See* Swallowtail: Fluted

forest, 78, 101, 160, 176, 188, 196, 255, 271, 345, 378, 394; beech, 188, 425; cove, 98, 202; deciduous/hardwood, 267, 394, 406, 419, 427; oak-hickory, 143

Formica spp. *See* ant: Wood

frass chain, 5, *235, 236, 239, 342, 343*

fritillary, 216, 245, 258; Aphrodite, 447; Diana, *264–69,* 309, 389, 433; Great Spangled, *270–75,* 389, 433; Greater, 10, 16, 216, 258, 270, 388–89; Gulf, *217, 244–51,* 258, 431; Meadow, 447; Variegated, 258–63, *259, 260, 261, 262, 263,* 432.

frogfruit, *65, 107,* 332, *334,* 401, 440

Frost, Robert, 196

Frosted Elfin. *See* elfin: Frosted

fugitive species, 128

Furanocoumarin, 28

Gamochaeta. See cudweed

garden bean, 182, 401

Garlic-Mustard, 101, 401

Gatrelle, Ron, 325, 370, 374

Gattinger's Prairie-Clover. *See* clover:
    Gattinger's Prairie-Clover

Gaylussacia. See huckleberry

Georgia, 59, 151, 169, 325, 330

Georgia Satyr. *See* satyr: Georgia

Giant Cane. *See* cane: Giant

Giant Ragweed. *See* ragweed: Giant

Giant Swallowtail. *See* swallowtail: Giant

Glassberg, Jeffrey, 378

glasswort, 190, *191*, 401, 425

Glaucopsyche lygdamus: *lygdamus*
    couperi (*see* silvery blue: "Northern");
    lygdamus lygdamus (*see* silvery blue:
    Appalachain-Native). *See also* silvery
    blue

glucosinolate, 61, 105

glycoside, 246; cardiac, 19, 215, 222,
    229; cyanogenic, 246, 255; iridoid,
    312, 332

goatweed, 340, 401, 441. *See also*
    Croton

Goatweed Leafwing. *See* leafwing:
    Goatweed

goldenrod, 134, 178, 184, *257, 294*, 401

Gorgone Checkerspot. *See* checkerspot:
    Gorgone

gossamer-wings, 115–207

Gosse, Philip Henry, *ii*, iii, ix, xiii, 9, 27,
    34, 35, 54, 245, 287, 303, 352, 382, 393

granite outcrop, 154, 374

grass, 3, 131, 215, 216, 345, 348, 360,
    361, 362, 364, 366, 370, 378, *379, 382,*
    387, 388, 389, *390*, 441, 442, 443,
    444; Bermuda, 364, 399; bluestem,
    365, 367, 368, 371, 385, 388, 399,
    446; Carpet, 364, 400; Cogon, 395,
    400; Eastern Bottlebrush, 348, 400;
    family (Poaceae), 441, 442, 443, 444,
    446; Japanese Stilt, 348, 366, 401;
    Slender Spikegrass, 360, 402; St.
    Augustine, 364, 403; Switchgrass,
    388, 403; White Cutgrass, 348, 403;
    Witch, 403

Gray Hairstreak. *See* hairstreak: Gray

Great Purple Hairstreak. *See* hairstreak:
    Great Purple

Great Southern White. *See* white: Great
    Southern

Great Spangled Fritillary. *See* fritillary:
    Great Spangled

greater fritillary. *See* fritillary: greater.

groundsel, 231, 401

Groundsel-Tree, *227, 228*, 401

Gulf Coast Swallow-Wort, 229, 230, 401

Gulf Fritillary. *See* fritillary: Gulf

habitat generalist, 80, 106, 176, 287, 314

habitat specialist, 144, 206, 208, 378

hackberry, *5*, 215, 219, 276, 278, 280,
    282, 283, 284, 285, 303; Southern,
    276, 403

Hackberry Emperor. *See* emperor:
Hackberry

hairpencil, 215, 229, *231*

hairstreak, 6, 8, 115, 116, 133, 138, 142;
Banded, 142–*43*, 418; Coral, 136–*37*,
417; Early, 188–*89*, 425; Edwards',
138–41, *139, 140–41*, 418; Gray, *117*,
180–83, 192, 424; Great Purple,
132–35, *132, 134, 135*, 417; Hessel's,
156–59, *157, 159*, 421; Hickory, 447;
Juniper, *154–55*, 156, 420; King's,
144–45, *419*; "Northern" Oak, 149,
150, 151, 402; Oak, 150–53, *152, 153*,
402, 403, 420; Red-Banded, 176–79,
188, 423; "Southern" Oak, *151*, 403;
Striped, 146–49, *147, 148, 149*, 419;
White-M, 184–87, *185, 186, 187*, 424.
See also Satyrium

Hairy Angelica, 28, *29, 31*, 401

Harvester, 115, 116, *118–21*, 415

hawthorn, 146, 182, 401

Heartleaf Aster. *See* aster: Heartleaf

heath, 160, 401; family (Ericaceae), 146,
160, 401, 419, 421, 422

Hedyloidea, 2

Helianthus. See sunflower

heliconia, 216, 245, 252, 253, 255. *See
also* longwing

Heliconius charithonia. See longwing:
Zebra

Helicta Satyr. *See* satyr: Helicta

heliotrope, 231, 401

Heliotropium. See heliotrope

Hemiargus ceraunus: See blue: Ceraunus

Henry's Elfin. *See* elfin: Henry's

Hercules'-Club. *See* Southern Prickly-Ash

Hermeuptychia sosybius. See satyr: Carolina

Hesperiidae, 2

Hessel's Hairstreak. *See* hairstreak:
Hessel's

hibernaculum, *235, 236, 240–41*

hibiscus, *89*, 182, 401, 402

hickory, 142, 143, 170, 182, 401, 419

Hickory Hairstreak. *See* hairstreak:
Hickory

hilltopping, 299

hog, feral, 380, 396, 400

Hogwort, *341, 342*, 401

Hop Merchant, 310

hops, 182, 310, 401

Hoptree, *35, 37*, 39, 401, 407

Horrid Thistle. *See* thistle: Horrid

Horse-Sugar, 144, *145*, 171, 401, 419

huckleberry, 146, 160, 401

Humulus lupulus. See hops

Ilex opaca. See American Holly

indigo: False, 84, *85*, 401, 412; Wild, 164,
403, 422

International Lepidoptera Survey, The
(TILS), 373, 374

International Paper Company, 158

iridoid glycoside. *See* glycoside: iridoid

Itea virginica. See Virginia Sweetspire

Jackson County, 41, 360

Japanese Stilt Grass. *See* grass:
Japanese Stilt

mallow, 182, 290, 401; family (Malvaceae), 435

Malvaceae. *See* mallow: family

Marine Blue. *See* blue: Marine

Maypop, 245, 251. *See also* passion-flower

Meadow Fritillary. *See* fritillary: Meadow

Medicago sativa. *See* alfalfa

Megiso: *M. cymela* (*see* satyr: Little Wood-Satyr); *M. cymela* viola (*see* satyr: "Viola's" Wood-Satyr)

Melilotus: *M. officinalis* (*see* clover: Yellow Sweet-Clover). *See also* clover

metalmark, 10, 208–13; Little, 208, *209*, 210–13, *210*, *212*, 428

Mexico, 223, 292, 405

Microstegium vimineum. *See* grass: Japanese Stilt

migration (dispersal or seasonal movement) 29, 70, 84, 215, *227*, 229

Mikania scandens. *See* Climbing Hempvine

milkweed, 54, 129, 131, 136, 146, 178, 182, 188, 215, 222, 223, 229, 231, 267, 268, 270, 274, 294, *318*, 401, 402, 429, 430, 433; Butterfly, 1, 136, *137*, 138, *140–41*, 142, *143*, *180*, 214, 217, 223, *224–25*, *237*, *264*, *316*, 336, *337*, 400, 417; Common, *18*, 129, *274–75*, 400; family (Asclepiadaceae), 229, 429, 430; Swamp, *193*, 223, 403

mimicry, 8, 9, 18, 19, 42, 340

mimicry ring, 18

Mississippi, 82, 160, 356, 380

Mitchell's Satyr. *See* satyr: Mitchell's

Mobile County, 156, 394

mock bishopweed, 28, 401

monarch, 6, 9, 125, 182, 222–27, *222*, *224–25*, *226*, *227*, 229, 231, 234, 238, 241, 292, 429, 431

Morella. *See* wax-myrtle

moth, 1, 2, 155, 210

Mountain-Laurel, *40*, 160, *162*, 401

mountain-mint, 178, 401

Mourning Cloak, 298–301, 436

Multiflora Rose. *See* rose: Multiflora

mustard, 60, 94, 102, 105, 107, 113; Chinese, *104*, 400; family (Brassicaceae), 99, 102, 111, 401, 413, 414, 415. *See also* Crucifer

Myrmecophily, 115, 190. *See also* ant: attendant

Nathalis iole. *See* sulphur: Dainty

nature conservancy, 158

NatureServe, 164, 166

nectary, 3, 92, 134, 255; extrafloral, 92

Neonympha: *N. areolatus* (*see* satyr: Georgia); *N. helicta* (*see* satyr: Helicta); *N. mitchellii* (*see* satyr: Mitchell's)

Neptunia. *See* puff

nettle, 294, 303, 309, 402, 437; False, 4, 294, *295*, 309, *311*, 400, 437; family (Urticaceae), 436, 437; Stinging, 295, 403

New England Aster. *See* aster: New England

New York Aster. *See* aster: New York

Newcomer's organ, 115, 190, 199

352–55, 353, 354, 442; Northern, 348–51, 349, 350, 442; Southern, 344–47, 344, 346, 347, 352, 353, 441

pencil-flower, 64, 402, 409; Side-Beak, 64, 402

Perry County, 333

Persea: *P. borbonia* (*see* redbay); *P. palustrus* (*see* redbay: Swamp). *See* redbay

Phaon Crescent. *See* crescent: Phaon

pheromone, 63, 70, 229

Phlox, 34, 160, 161, 169, 402

Phoebis: *P. philea*, 447, *P. sennae* (*see* sulphur: Cloudless)

Phyciodes: *P. phaon* (*see* crescent: Phaon); *P. tharos* (*see* crescent: Pear

Phyla. *See* frogfruit

phytochemical, 3, 5, 19, 123, 133, 238, 255

pierid, 60, 61, 82, 94, 98, 105, 110

Pieridae, 60–61. *See also* sulphur: White

Pieris: *P. rapae* (*see* white: Cabbage); *P. virginiensis* (*see* white: West Virginia)

Pinaceae. *See* pine: family

pine, 160, 171, 172, 173, 174, 180, 370, 374, 394, 402; family (Pinaceae), 423; hard, 172; Loblolly, 173, 401, 424, 429; Longleaf, 370, 394, 401; plantation, 173, 394; savanna, 180, 370, 374, 428, 444; Virginia, 173, 403

pine elfin. *See* elfin: Eastern Pine

Pinus: *P. palustris* (*see* pine: Longleaf); *P. taeda* (*see* pine: Loblolly); *P. virginiana* (*see* pine: Virginia). *See* pine

pipevine, 8, 19, 20, 21, 402, 405

Pipevine Swallowtail. *See* swallowtail: Pipevine

pitcher plant/pitcher plant bog, 210, 370, 371, 403

Plantain-Leaf Pussytoes. *See* pussytoes: Plaintain-Leaf

plum: flowering, 25, 27, 171, 172, 287, 401; wild, 42, 45, 47, 49, 178, 404, 417

pollen/pollen-eating, 3, 152, 160, 169, 196, 215, 245, 253

Polygonaceae. *See* Buckwheat family

Polygonia, 303; *P. comma* (*see* anglewing: Comma); *P. faunus* (*see* anglewing: Green); *P. interrogationis* (*see* Question Mark)

Polygonum. *See* knotweed

Poorman's Pepperwort, 106, 107, 108, 112, 402, 414, 415

Popcorn-Tree, 400; *See also* Chinese Tallow-Tree

Populus. *See* Cottonwood

Prairie, xiii, 28, 54, 82, 84, 180, 342, 388, 412; Blackland, 82, 154

Prairie-Clover. *See* clover: Prairie-Clover

praying mantis, 5, 7, 72, 402

privet, 146, 404; Chinese, 395, 400

Prunus. *See* plum

Ptelea trifoliate. *See* Hoptree

pteridine, 60

Ptilimnium. *See* mock bishopweed

puddling/puddle club, 40, 41, 47, 66, 71, 72, 80, 116, 173, 196, 218, 236, 280, 306, 316

puff, 71, 72, 402

wood ant. *See* ant: wood

Wood-Satyr: Little (*See* satyr: Little
    Wood-Satyr; "Viola's" (*see* "Viola's"
    Wood-Satyr)

Woolly aphid. *See* aphid: Woolly

Woolly Croton. *See* croton: Woolly

Woolly Dutchman's-Pipe. *See* pipevine

Wright, David, 40

Yellow Passion-Flower. *See* passion-
    flower: Yellow

Yellow Sweet-Clover. *See* clover: Yellow
    Sweet-Clover

Zanthaxylum clava-herculis. See
    Southern Prickly-Ash

Zebra Longwing. *See* longwing: Zebra

Zebra Swallowtail. *See* swallowtail:
    Zebra

Zerene cesonia. See Southern Dogface

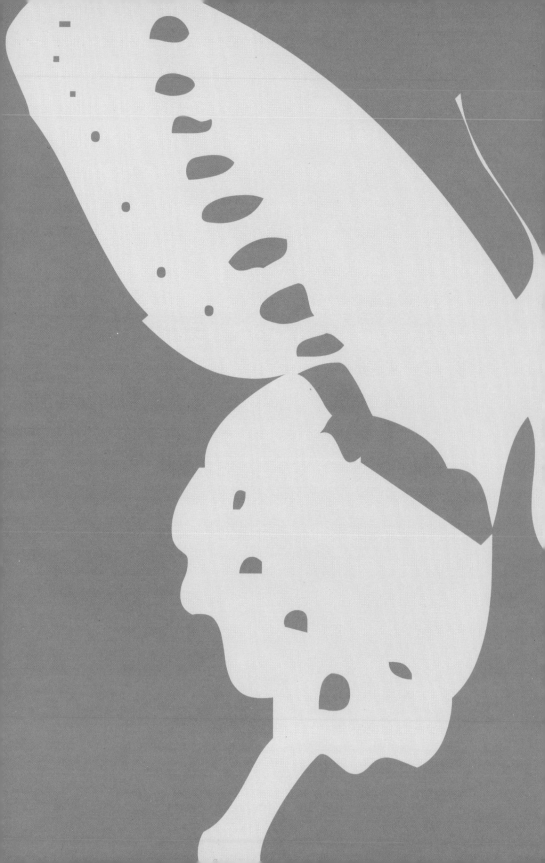